Wired Differently

A Teacher's Guide to Understanding Sensory Processing Challenges

by Keriann Wilmot, OTR/L

www.gryphonhouse.com

Copyright

Published by Gryphon House, Inc.
P. O. Box 10, Lewisville, NC 27023
800.638.0928; 877.638.7576 [fax]
Visit us on the web at www.gryphonhouse.com.

Library of Congress Control Number: 2020933513

Bulk Purchase

Gryphon House books are available for special premiums and sales promotions as well as for fund-raising use. Special editions or book excerpts also can be created to specifications. For details, call 800.638.0928.

Disclaimer

Gryphon House, Inc., cannot be held responsible for damage, mishap, or injury incurred during the use of or because of activities in this book. Appropriate and reasonable caution and adult supervision of children involved in activities and corresponding to the age and capability of each child involved are recommended at all times. Do not leave children unattended at any time. Observe safety and caution at all times.

Table of Contents

Introduction

Being an early childhood educator to children ages three to five is one of the most fun and exciting jobs I can imagine. Children this age are just adorable little sponges soaking up all the information the world can offer as they expand their knowledge and language, while they play and engage in the types of fun-filled activities that adults envy!

Preschoolers love to play with vehicles and dollhouses, and they are also learning to color while holding a crayon, engaging in painting and crafting activities, talking about the weather, learning to go to the bathroom by themselves, and learning how to dress themselves for outdoor playtime. At this age, they learn about colors, shapes, letters, and numbers as they are receiving their first introduction to academics and education.

Starting the school year can be a challenge for any teacher, but especially for early childhood teachers. Children at this age are curious, excited, and learning the classroom routines. For most children, learning the rules of preschool takes time and practice, but with repetition and structure they do; every day is a little easier. Confidence blooms as children develop new skills. But what about those children who struggle in preschool?

Ava, Zion, and Min-jun

Let's meet three early childhood students in three different early childhood environments.

Ava

Ava is a four-year-old girl in a private child-care setting where she participates in a structured preschool opportunity in the morning. Ava's beautiful long hair, which she will not let anyone cut or put into a ponytail, is a straggly mess. It frequently covers her eyes and interferes with her play as she struggles to see through it. She likes organized and structured play activities that involve color sorting. However, she always wants to play according to her own agenda and does not like to follow the teacher's rules. Ava orders other children around when playing. She may scream when she is mad if they don't participate her way. Transitions to activities she does not like, such as classroom art projects or circle time, can lead to yelling, crying, and tantrums or running away to another part of the classroom. Children and teachers who try to engage with her in an effort to help her may be met with lashing out through hitting, kicking, pushing, and yelling. Ava refuses to sit on the carpet with her peers at circle time and is often found playing with a toy on her own at the back of the room. Redirecting her to the circle-time carpet square leads to her flopping on the floor and more outbursts. Ava frequently refuses to put on coats or other clothing with fasteners prior to outdoor time. She dislikes using the restroom at school because she is terrified of the automatic toilet flusher; consequently, she is often constipated. She has a limited diet of foods she likes to eat. She does not use utensils properly, shoving food into her mouth and taking bites that are too large. Rest time has become a significant challenge, as she is not able to settle down on her mat to fall asleep; her wakefulness leads to disruptive and inappropriate behaviors as she tries to leave her mat and play with toys in the room. Ava has not been successful with building friendships and relationships in the classroom. She is often dressed in the same cotton, loose-fitting clothing, and she prefers wearing old sneakers or winter boots, even when they are too small or out of season.

While Ava is able to speak and communicate, she struggles to use her language effectively to share her frustrations. Instead, in an attempt to get her needs met, she resorts to physical actions such as hitting or yelling. Ava is not responsive to her teachers' attempts to help her, and other students are beginning to copy her behavior. The director has met with her parents multiple times about her disruptive and unsafe behavior and is considering asking her parents to find another program.

Zion

Zion is an energetic four-year-old boy in a private, half-day, morning preschool program at his community church. At circle time he is unable to remain on his carpet square, lying on the carpet, frequently changing his position, and bumping into other students who complain that he is in their personal space and that he is hurting them. When sitting in a chair at the table, Zion rocks back and forth in it unsafely and prefers to stand at the table to complete his work. When playing with toys, he bangs them together forcefully, often breaking his creations or those of his peers. When building with toys, he struggles to use the right force to attach pieces correctly and is often frustrated. During computer time, Zion refuses to wear headphones. In the classroom environment, he covers his ears and complains that the noises are too loud. He speaks so quickly at times it can be hard to understand what he is saying. Zion brings the exact same lunch every day and is very particular about what he eats and how he eats it. Yet, for some reason, he puts all sorts of toys in his mouth and frequently bites and chews on his clothing and other classroom items. Playdough and sand-and-water play are his favorite classroom activities, but he avoids sticky or messy painting. He frequently complains that his hands are dirty and requests wipes to clean them off. Zion's parents tell his teacher each morning how difficult it is for him to fall asleep at bedtime and that he was up several times during the night. Other teachers have wondered whether Zion could have an attention disorder that is affecting his ability to learn new skills, because he's constantly on the go and has difficulty remembering any of his letters or numbers.

Min-jun

Min-jun is a sweet but very quiet and shy little boy. Each day he struggles to say goodbye to his parents and transition into the preschool classroom routine. However, he eventually settles in and takes his spot on the carpet for circle time. He remains seated in the correct spot but often can be seen chewing on his shirt during circle time. As his teacher reads stories aloud, he does not appear to be following along. He needs a little bit more time to process a question before he answers, but he is able to effectively remember details of the stories. While Min-jun occasionally needs some reminders and cueing, he participates in classroom routines appropriately. His parents have shared that he is struggling at home with a lot of behaviors. Getting to school in the morning is a huge stress for the family and a daily hurdle for Min-jun, as he takes a long time to wake up and get moving in the morning and then does not want to wear certain clothing items. His refusal can lead to intense meltdowns before leaving for school. When he arrives home at the end of the day, he can also be challenging and has frequent tantrums. His parents wonder if he is exhibiting the same behaviors at school. They are worried about his ability to learn and participate with his peers, but for the most part, he is succeeding at school without any major issues.

Despite the repetition, routine, and practice, and even though peers are making progress, children like Ava, Min-jun, and Zion continue to demonstrate more frustration. Instead of each day being easier, it's harder and a lot more challenging for them, their parents, their teachers, and their peers. Situations in the classroom cause meltdowns. The idea of transitioning to the carpet to sit "crisscross applesauce on their pockets" is met with resistance and tantrums.

You may have experienced similar situations in your own classroom. Even though you've agonized over choosing the best circle-time book ever, you can't figure out why, as you read a book, one little girl is refusing to sit with her peers, preferring to play alone at another corner of the classroom. Most of the class cheers with excitement over playdough, sand, or slime in the sensory table, while another student stands there screeching, both hands held high in the air as if it's the worst thing ever, refusing to look at or even touch the substance at all. Any transition to a nonpreferred activity, including mealtimes and nap times, might be easy for these children one day, but on another could lead to running away, hitting their friends, kicking their feet, and yelling. Making new friends is a struggle for them; other children who approach them could encounter an unpredictable scream, swat, hit, or kick.

If you have a child like Ava, Zion, or Min-jun in your classroom, you recognize the challenges.

The strategies in your teacher toolbox just aren't making a difference. Each and every day in the classroom has become a struggle. While you know certain activities might make the child happy and some days are great, other days the child seems to disrupt and derail the entire classroom. You've begun to wonder whether you'll make it through the year together and meet every academic target. You, the other teachers, and the children are walking on eggshells, trying not to set this child off.

You've reached out to the parents to find out if this behavior occurs at home too. How can you share your concerns with the parents? You aren't sure what is going on, but something does not seem right. Some of the child's behaviors have become unsafe and even required incident reports. Others have required a trip to the director's office and a phone call home to the parents. Perhaps, as you have reached out to friends, perused websites, and engaged in seminars to try to make sense of these behaviors, you've stumbled across the term *sensory processing disorder* (SPD). Could this be what is making it difficult for your student to participate and learn in your classroom? And if so, what can you, as a preschool teacher, do?

First, know that you are not alone. Many of your colleagues teach children like Ava, Zion, and Min-jun, and they, too, struggle with similar issues. Second, it's important to understand that what you see these children doing is not something they choose to do; it is their way of communicating to you that something isn't right. Finally, there are solutions, which you'll read about in this book. Helping children with sensory issues involves offering fun, child-friendly tools and experiences—often through play—that can make a world of difference in a child's school day.

How This Book Is Organized

In the first chapter, you'll learn what SPD is, how it is recognized, and what services are available for children with SPD. Chapter 2 covers how children with SPD present in the early childhood classroom; how occupational therapists can help; and what your role is in getting assistance for these children, including how to communicate with families. In chapters 3, 4, and 5, you'll learn how to set up a sensory-friendly classroom and read about tips, tools, strategies, and even apps to help you teach children with SPD. The book concludes with specific examples of accommodations for children with different sensory issues.

My hope is that this book will help you understand your role, learn some new strategies, and formulate a plan of action. Then, you will have the tools to help a child who has SPD be as independent and successful as possible, even if she is only in your classroom for a short period of time and moves on to another program.

My Qualifications for Writing This Book

I have worked as an occupational therapist in public schools, outpatient clinics, and residential hospital schools for children. I also have offered in-home intensive services for children in a birth-to-three early intervention program. In birth-to-three, I have spent many hours cross-legged on living room floors alongside teachers, speech therapists, and physical therapists, exploring ways to help children with all types of special needs meet their developmental milestones. I drove almost 40,000 miles my first year as an occupational therapist, seeing children at their homes and schools and spending several thousand dollars buying toys, games, and other activities to use with the vast array of children I was helping.

Over the years, I've worked in other early intervention programs and at a children's hospital alongside neuropsychologists, nurse practitioners, neonatologists, psychiatrists, speech pathologists, and physical therapists, helping children with significant medical issues. I have worked in the public school system evaluating children to determine whether they are eligible to receive occupational therapy services at school. I've spent countless hours observing students and educating teachers on accommodations and strategies to help children feel more successful in their classrooms, using many of the recommendations and strategies you will read in this book.

I have noticed that, over the last twenty years, it has become harder and harder for children to succeed in preschool. Year after year, the number of referrals has increased, and the issues children are having in the classroom seem to be more and more complicated. How is it possible that, for an alarming number of children, the preschool classroom is not the fun, productive learning environment teachers and parents hope it will be? Often, families are asked to unenroll their children, but they quickly learn that a new environment without the proper supports yields the same disappointing and frustrating results.

More parents have begun referring their children for specialized services, as they hear from their children's private-school teachers about incidents regarding unsafe behaviors. Often, upon transition to a specialized program where sensory needs and learning styles are met in a smaller environment with more-skilled teachers and access to supports and accommodations, children no longer exhibit the behaviors they had shown previously. They are thriving and learning in the new environment.

I'm truly thankful to all of the families who agreed to let me enter their homes and work with their children. I'm grateful to teachers who have the ability to keep children learning for several hours a day, because I truly understand how difficult it can be to keep children motivated to learn. I'm thankful for opportunities to collaborate alongside parents, teachers, and medical professionals. When everyone involved in a child's day-to-day life is positive and focused on what they can do to help make a difference, families' lives change for the better. I hope that you benefit from the support of occupational therapists who want the best for children's preschool success and education.

Sensory Processing Disorder

The Senses

Most people know about the traditional five senses: sight, smell, touch, hearing, and taste. While it might not be something that you think about consciously, every day our brain uses these senses to process information from the world around us. Multisensory learning is the basis for how children are educated in an early childhood classroom. Children's senses are engaged throughout the day as they learn and explore.

Children use their sense of sight to observe the teacher demonstrating new skills for matching colors, forming letters, or imitating actions of a new song. Some might become aware of the smell of disinfectant wipes used to clean the classroom, while others don't notice the scent of air fresheners or diffusers. Paints, sand, and other sensory textures are available to explore with their sense of touch. Noises surround them in the form of music played during movement breaks and transitions, loud banging from children building and toppling structures in the block corner, the flush of the toilet in the restroom, and the chatter of children working at different centers with their peers. While certainly taste is mostly reserved for snacks and mealtimes, I'm sure you've encountered a child who just can't help sampling the paint or playdough, while others nibble or mouth blocks, toys, and other manipulatives.

In addition to these five, three more senses are important to understand: proprioception, vestibular sense, and interoception.

- *Proprioception:* a sense of body awareness; knowing how to control and coordinate our muscles and joints during everyday activities using the right force and speed
- *Vestibular sense:* our sense of balance, located in our inner ear
- *Interoception:* a newly identified sense that helps body parts communicate to the brain that a person might be hungry, tired, or have to use the restroom

Now let's add these three additional senses and see how they affect a child in the classroom. In terms of proprioception, children need to develop an appropriate sense of body awareness as they move about the classroom, so they can maintain boundaries and avoid invading another's personal space. It's important to regulate the force of their muscles for activities, so they can squeeze the appropriate amount of glue onto a piece of paper or regulate their force so the play structure they've worked hard to build doesn't get knocked over.

Then, with their sense of vestibular sense and use of movement, children travel from one center to another with the appropriate speed, and they transition from sitting to standing at circle time during music and movement. Interoception is a sense we are learning more about. The body's organs contain receptors that are crucial for skills such as digestion, hunger, pain, and knowing when to use the restroom in time without having an accident. It can be difficult for children to perform if their systems are not working efficiently or if there is an issue with the neurological system integrating and coordinating all of this sensory input over the course of the day.

When these systems are not working in harmony, many children will overreact or underreact to the information their brains are receiving, which can cause any number of issues in the classroom. Think about what happens when you are driving a car and hear a fire engine's siren. You have learned in that situation not to panic but to slow the vehicle and pull over. But if the siren triggers a fight-or-flight reaction, you may panic and speed up unsafely, because your sensory system is overwhelmed.

All children need to develop safe, appropriate responses to stimuli, but children who struggle with SPD have a hard time reacting appropriately to everyday sensory stimuli. Instead, they respond with atypical, inappropriate, or unexpected reactions. Children with SPD often need help to work through these obstacles, because their reactions tend to be much more intense and challenging than those of their peers. They need help and support to develop self-regulation.

Self-regulation is awareness of one's own emotions and activity level, figuring out behavioral strategies needed to be successful, and advocating for those strategies. Under the guidance or supervision of a teacher or parent, children can learn how to self-regulate. Children with SPD often have unique classroom behaviors that are seen as inappropriate. However, if you watch carefully and ask questions, you'll soon realize that maybe the child who is sitting with his feet up on a desk or is rocking back in his chair is attempting to self-regulate so he can pay attention to classroom instructions. Closely observe what children are doing in the classroom and what they are asking for. Set limits, boundaries, and classroom expectations, but also be responsive to children's needs. If a child is asking to take a break to get his wiggles out, and it's an appropriate request to get work done rather than to avoid it, honor that request. That child has identified a strategy that might be crucial to his classroom success.

Sensory Processing Disorder Defined

Sensory processing disorder (SPD) was originally known as sensory integration dysfunction. Children who have these unique challenges are also referred to as having sensory issues or sensory processing issues. For those who might be hearing these terms and names for the first time, SPD is a very broad neurophysiological condition. The main term does not really give any hints as to what the issues might be or how severe they are, since not every child with SPD reacts and responds in the same way.

The late A. Jean Ayres, PhD, OTR, was an occupational therapist, educational psychologist, and researcher who first identified these challenges and this disorder in the late 1970s. Her book *Sensory Integration and the Child* has served as a reference and a handbook for those learning about the disorder. In her book, Dr. Ayres uses an excellent analogy to help readers understand SPD. She suggests they envision having a traffic cop in the brain. When information from the environment enters the brain through one or more of our senses, the traffic cop has a very important job: to determine what to do with that information before making an appropriate response.

Other pioneers in sensory-integration research include Lucy Jane Miller, PhD, OTR/L, and Carol Kranowitz. Dr. Miller is the founder of the STAR Institute for Sensory Processing Disorder, an organization created to offer research, education, and treatment for individuals with SPD. Ms. Kranowitz was a music, movement, and drama teacher who worked with preschoolers. Her popular book *The Out-of-Sync Child* is an excellent resource for parents seeking to learn about sensory processing disorder and to find strategies to assist with sensory integration.

SPD is an individual's inability to control or coordinate all the sensory input from the world that is entering their system through their senses. This results in feelings of being overwhelmed and overstimulated, which are exhibited as many different types of "unwanted behaviors." Children who struggle with SPD have a hard time succeeding and coping when completing everyday life activities and routines, especially when they are required to participate in and focus on academic tasks as part of a large-group environment in school. Note that sensory processing issues do not discriminate based upon age. Because school is often the first time children are asked to participate and perform in new, challenging environments outside of their homes, sensory issues are often identified in school-aged children; however, infants and adults can struggle with SPD as well.

SPD is the inability of an individual to control or coordinate all the sensory input from the world that is entering their system through their senses.

It has been reported by the STAR Institute that one in twenty people in the general population may be affected by SPD. A 2013 study by Julia Owen and colleagues at Benioff Children's Hospital at the University of California, San Francisco, was the first to identify structural differences in the white matter of the brain with children who have sensory processing issues. It is not known what causes SPD, but of those with diagnoses such as attention deficit hyperactivity disorder (ADHD) and autism, the incidence of SPD may even be higher than one in twenty. Genetics could also play a factor in diagnosis. What we know for sure is that we need continued research to truly understand this complicated disorder.

Everyone has sensory preferences that are part of who they are, and every human being can face sensory challenges. For example, you might not like the scratchiness of tags and seams in your clothes, so you buy soft clothes without seams and cut the tags out. Another person may absolutely refuse to mix their corn into their mashed potatoes at Thanksgiving dinner, keeping each food perfectly separated on the plate. But when a child has so many preferences that it impacts his daily functioning, we can identify that there may be sensory processing disorder.

Sensory processing disorder is complicated. It is a self-regulation disorder that is affected by a child's arousal level. Thus, an overstimulating event or situation that occurred hours or even days before may affect a child's energy level and participation at a later time. And a child's inconsistencies in behavior can make SPD very difficult to identify and extremely frustrating for caregivers who want to help. Why does a noise, a texture, or lighting lead to a major meltdown today but not tomorrow? Identifying SPD can be even more complicated because some children perform better in certain environments and struggle in others. While many children thrive on the structure and consistency of school programs and teachers, others function better at home where there is less stimulation, far away from the sights, sounds, and experiences that continually bombard their systems in a classroom. A child's inconsistent responses can also lead to a lot of animosity between home and school, especially when a child's sensory issues at school can be so disruptive to the classroom that they prompt multiple discussions with the parents regarding safety.

One of the most common questions teachers, parents, and even therapists ask themselves when working with young children who may have sensory processing disorder is, "Is this a sensory disorder, or is it just bad behavior?" Unfortunately, this question is not easily answered. SPD can be identified through the symptoms and behaviors a child exhibits. While certain behaviors certainly need to be managed, teachers should know that this is usually a situation that is out of the child's control.

Children with sensory processing issues are not planning on misbehaving. They have formed inappropriate coping mechanisms in response to situations that are occurring in the environment. They are unable to respond appropriately to all the information entering and exiting their neurological systems. They need a teacher's help, calm demeanor, and guidance to be redirected to learning activities in a positive way. The teacher's yelling, scolding, or frustration shown in a negative way are counterproductive.

The Occupational Therapist's Role in Helping Young Children with SPD

An occupational therapist (OT) is a rehabilitation professional who may work with individuals of all ages to promote their activities of daily living. For example, families with an adult family member who has been in an accident or suffered neurological trauma such as a stroke likely have met with an OT. The OT is tasked with helping their loved one return to his activities of daily living. The OT's challenge might include teaching the family member how to rebuild the strength and coordination necessary to complete activities he was able to do independently before the accident or illness, such as brushing his teeth, getting dressed, manipulating fasteners on clothing, tying his shoelaces, washing dishes, and cooking a meal.

Pediatric occupational therapy is a specialty area of the occupational therapy profession. In addition to understanding sensory processing, pediatric OTs are well versed in the typical path of early childhood development, especially with regard to gross- and fine-motor milestones as they relate to daily living or self-care skills. An occupational therapist who works in the early childhood environment is skilled at knowing at what age it is typical for children to be able to climb up the playground equipment or hold a crayon with their fingertips when drawing a circle. A pediatric OT knows how to teach children with special needs how to use scissors to cut along different lines and how to button buttons, tie their shoelaces, use a spoon, or cut with a knife. Typical gross- and fine-motor development occur over a wide range of timeframes because everyone learns at different rates. The OT with early childhood experience knows when children should reach typical educational and self-help milestones and is able to understand when a child's inability to complete a task is not typical for his age. After completing an evaluation, the OT designs an individualized therapy or intervention plan for the child to help him learn those new skills and perform at the same level as his peers.

Services might be provided in any number of settings, including outpatient settings or the child's home or day care. If a child is struggling at school, additional services can be provided by the public

school system for free, if the child meets very specific eligibility criteria. Not only are OTs helpful with advancing the skills of the child, they are also skilled at educating family members, caregivers, and teachers, so the child can be successful in all aspects of his day.

The OT will determine whether a child has enough signs and symptoms to indicate that sensory processing disorder is impacting his day-to-day life experiences and ability to learn, socialize, and participate. The OT will then determine whether the child requires regular therapy sessions and/or interventions to overcome these issues or is simply struggling with issues that are part of normal development. An OT who has advanced knowledge of sensory processing issues is able to look at all the signs and symptoms a child is experiencing, relate them to child development, and determine whether the situation is mild, moderate, or severe. Based upon the child's presentation, there may be certain accommodations or modifications to the daily routine and classroom environment that are more effective than others.

Types of Sensory Processing Disorders

There are three different subtypes of sensory processing disorder:

- Sensory modulation disorder
- Sensory-based motor disorder
- Sensory discrimination disorder

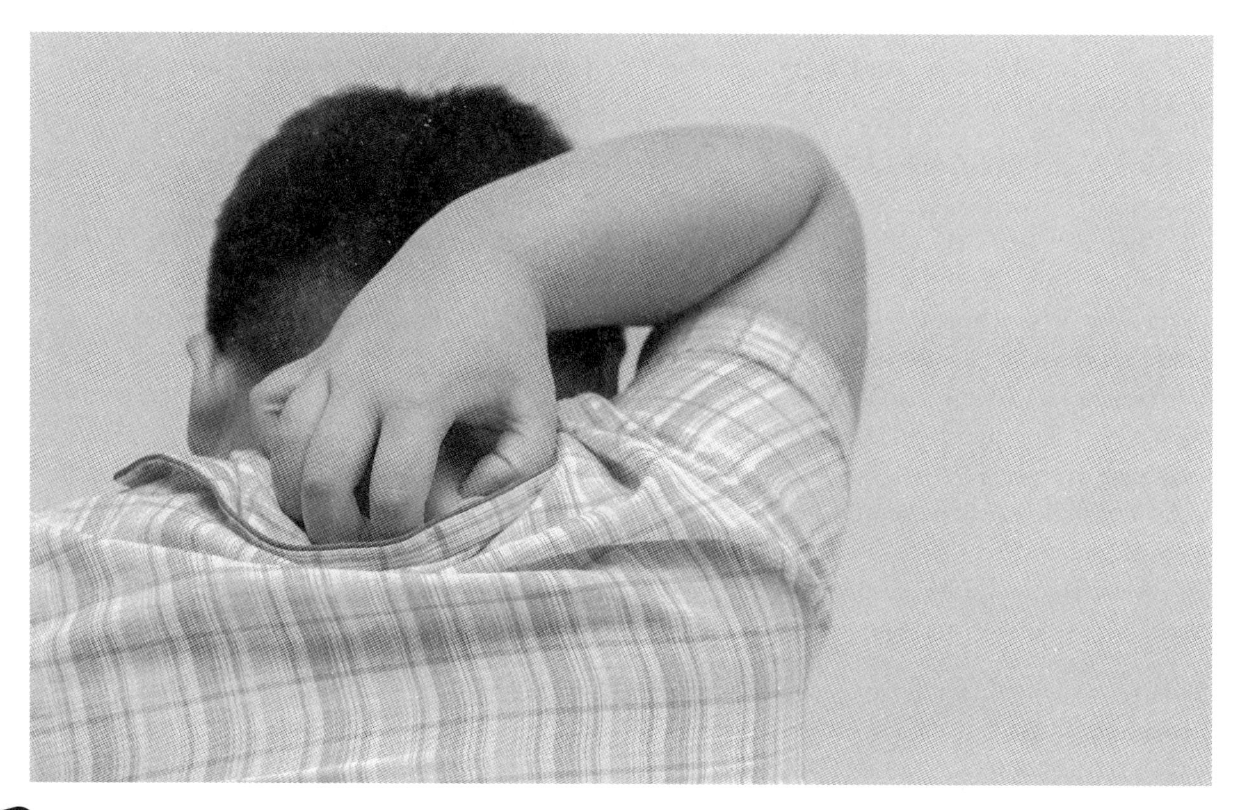

Sensory Modulation Disorder

Sensory modulation disorder can be described as an issue with self-regulation. This means that the brain has trouble adjusting to, recuperating from, and coping with all of the sensory input it receives throughout the day and from one day to another. According to the STAR Institute, there are three classifications within the sensory modulation disorder description, and children may display specific traits that place them in one of these subcategories:

- Sensory over-responsivity
- Sensory under-responsivity
- Sensory craving

A child with *sensory over-responsivity* reacts faster and more intensely to something most people don't find to be an issue in the first place. For example, the child may scream in pain from a minor bump. Many of these children are grossed out at the feel or look of textures such as food, paint, or toothpaste; some might refuse to touch or play with these substances altogether. Remember our discussion about Ava in the introduction? Ava is exhibiting sensory over-responsivity. She has issues with letting people cut or style her hair, listening to the sound of the toilet flushing, and wearing clothing that is not loose fitting and made of cotton. She also exhibits hitting, kicking, and pushing when others attempt to redirect her.

A child with *sensory underresponsivity* doesn't react at all to a stimulus, has a delayed response, or requires an intense amount of sensory input to feel it or register it. Children who are underresponsive to stimuli might be lethargic, subdued, or passive. In the description of Min-jun, at times he shows signs of sensory underresponsivity, when it takes his sensory system a bit of time to wake up in the morning. He also exhibits underresponsivity when he doesn't appear to be paying attention at circle time and has a delayed response to his teacher's questions.

A child who is identified as *sensory craving* has intense sensory needs. Often, the child is so driven that his behavior can be very unsafe and dangerous. Sensory cravers are runners, movers, shakers, crashers, and bangers. Their bull-in-a-china-shop activity level makes it difficult for them to settle down in a classroom and to sit and pay attention for learning. Many wonder if these children also have ADHD.

Remember Zion? When he rocks back and forth in his chair, bangs toys forcefully, and mouths and chews on clothing, he is exhibiting behaviors of a child who is sensory craving.

In comparison to their peers, a child with a sensory modulation disorder has reactions that are more frequent and more intense than those of their peers. In addition, because the lasting effect of this stimulation is cumulative, stressful situations that occurred the day before can have a long-lasting negative impact on the child's sensory system for hours and even days at a time. Thus, it can be hard for many children to cope with transitions and changes in their world, long after you think the sensory incident is over.

So, imagine how a child with a sensory modulation disorder may be feeling in a sensory-stimulating environment, such as a busy classroom setting. If the "traffic cop" in the brain is not able to make sense of all the incoming information, the child's preferred coping mechanism may be either to avoid situations or to react in an inappropriate or atypical way, rather than as their peers do or as society expects them to.

Over my career, in many different educational settings that include both private and public-school preschool and day-care facilities, I've evaluated and worked with hundreds of children with SPD who have sensory modulation disorders. These children, in particular, struggle with learning the skills they need to participate successfully in preschool, such as attending to stories in circle time, transitioning to and performing center-based activities, participating in nonpreferred activities, remembering their letters, and socially engaging appropriately with peers in nonaggressive ways. But don't worry! There are strategies to help these children and to help you make the classroom the best learning environment it can be.

Sensory-Based Motor Disorder

The second type of sensory processing disorder is sensory-based motor disorder (SBMD).

For many reasons, some children do not possess the appropriate motor strength and coordination in their core abdominal muscles, arms, and hands. This can have a tremendous effect on their education and academics if they are simply unable to sit up for a period of time without support or struggle to hold a pencil or scissors correctly as they write their names or complete typical preschool activities such as gluing, painting, coloring, and cutting.

Children with a SBMD struggle with weakness, endurance, and muscle coordination. They often have issues with *dyspraxia*, commonly known as *motor planning*. Their inability to figure out or plan how to start, participate in, and complete a task accurately serves as a major factor in their inability to learn new tasks quickly. Dyspraxia can make learning complicated motor sequences such as skipping, tying shoelaces, and learning letter formation very challenging and can lead to frustration and task avoidance. A subtype of SBMS is postural disorder. Children with postural disorder struggle with coordination of their muscles and joints and are often described as being weak, clumsy, and exhibiting poor balance and endurance.

Sensory Discrimination Disorder

The third type of sensory processing disorder is sensory discrimination disorder. Children with sensory discrimination disorder have challenges organizing, distinguishing, and identifying the subtle differences in their sensory systems. For example, with regard to the tactile sense, a child may be unable to identify substances through only his sense of touch. When presented with rice and playdough, the child cannot tell the difference without looking. Children with visual-discrimination issues may not be able to distinguish various colors, shapes, or numbers. Children with auditory-discrimination issues may have difficulty localizing sound sources, such as listening to the teacher's instructions in a loud room full of children. These are only a few examples, but children can present with discrimination disorder in any one of their eight sensory systems.

Evaluation and Diagnosis of Sensory Processing Disorder

Many children enter preschool or day care without a formal diagnosis, but they may show signs of developmental delays when compared with their peers. Some children may enter the classroom setting with an identified diagnosis, such as autism. As disorders such as autism and ADHD are more widely understood, a parent may disclose to you that their child has been struggling. The parent may describe sensory issues but be unaware that there is a condition that matches these unique behaviors.

SPD is a type of disability that is evaluated and treated most effectively by a pediatric occupational therapist. Although as a teacher you are not able to clinically diagnose the situation, your input and relationship with the family is important in taking the next steps to get the child and yourself some much-needed help. Before we can share some strategies you can implement if you suspect a child is having issues with SPD, let's talk about how a pediatric occupational therapist makes an effective diagnosis through an evaluation, so you can understand how the process of determining eligibility for services works.

Understanding an Occupational-Therapy Evaluation

During an evaluation, OTs will watch the child participate in both structured and playful experiences, looking for how he reacts and responds. Along with clinical observations, parents and teachers may complete structured, standardized checklists that compare the child's performance at different ages with his peers. As long as caregivers and parents are reporting the child's participation appropriately, checklists, while subjective, are helpful in determining eligibility and offering some ideas on a place to start with a plan of care. Parents are also consulted regarding the child's performance with activities during day-to-day life. If services are requested at school, teachers may also be asked to share how the child is performing with his peers, how he interacts with classroom sensory materials, and whether he tolerates transitions and changes in classroom routines.

OTs have created standardized tests and checklists to help guide identification of SPD, as well as to determine the level at which children are functioning. Popular resources include the following:

- *The Sensory Profile 2* by Winnie Dunn, PhD, FAOTA: a standardized checklist parents and teachers fill out, which can be used for children from birth through age fourteen
- *Sensory Processing Measure* (SPM) by L. Diane Parham, PhD, OTR/L, FAOTA, and colleagues

These checklists ask caregivers to rate certain sensory behaviors and actions using responses of *always*, *frequently*, *occasionally*, or *never*. The scores are tallied and represented in standard scores with percentiles. They are then compared with statistical norms for the "average" person in the same age group. The results show the severity of the child's sensory issues and how the child's function relates to same-age peers.

These assessments are a great starting point to guide the beginning of treatment services and to use as a way to measure progress moving forward. However, not all caregivers, parents, and teachers understand the questions, nor are they all accurate reporters. Therefore, it is best practice to have the checklist filled out with the occupational therapist, who can ask detailed questions to gain the most information and relate it back to sensory processing.

There are many different types of non-standardized checklists that you can find online. These can help identify sensory needs, but the areas of concern should be evaluated by a professional occupational therapist who can determine the significance of the issues. Nonstandardized tools should be used only as indicators to pinpoint areas of need within specific senses.

What Is an SPD "Diagnosis"?

The *Diagnostic and Statistical Manual of Mental Disorders*, 5th edition (DSM-5), defines disorders to aid in diagnosis, treatment, and research. Whether SPD should be included in the DSM-5 has long been a controversial subject. Many feel that there is just not enough conclusive evidence and research regarding sensory processing and occupational therapy. Consequently, in the medical realm, there is not actually a formal diagnosis of SPD, as there are for specific conditions such as autism, Down syndrome, and cerebral palsy.

Occupational therapists are skilled at identifying symptoms and determining the degree of severity with which sensory issues are affecting a child's life, but OTs are not able to diagnose other common conditions such as ADHD or autism. Those conditions are usually diagnosed by a psychologist or neuropsychologist, after extensive testing. Not all children are referred to an occupational therapist first. Given that ADHD and autism include sensory issues as part of the diagnostic criteria, psychologists often make referrals to OTs too.

Families often wonder if a child can be diagnosed with SPD by itself, or if their child might have another disability, such as autism or ADHD, along with SPD. Common childhood diagnoses are important for early childhood teachers to learn about, because it's possible a child could be enrolled in a day-care or preschool setting for his first school experience without his family being aware that the child is not performing at the same level as his peers. (See "Common Disorders of Early Childhood that often Coexist in Children with SPD" on pages 18–22.) Sometimes the classroom teacher is the first person to identify that something is different with the child's learning style and abilities in comparison to his peers. There is no doubt that, after working with a lot of children over the years, an experienced professional will be able to spot the signs and symptoms of a child who is struggling in the classroom in comparison to his peer group.

Common Disorders of Early Childhood that often Coexist in Children with SPD

Doctors and psychologists provide a diagnosis using strict criteria shared in the DSM-5. This detailed manual helps effectively identify disorders through observing the presence of specific symptoms. While there is a lot of excellent information on the internet that can be used as a reference, it's still best to leave medical diagnoses to professionals.

- **Attention deficit hyperactivity disorder (ADHD):** a neurodevelopmental disorder that affects a child's attention and focus to learn new skills. ADHD is not usually diagnosed before the age of four but can be diagnosed at any age into adulthood. Hallmarks include the following characteristics:
    - » Inability to pay attention and focus on tasks, which leads to careless mistakes
    - » Hyperactive movements, including lots of running and climbing
    - » Inability to settle down to play or work for a period of time without being distracted
    - » Issues with organization
    - » Struggles with starting, persisting, and completing nonpreferred activities
    - » Excessive talking and interrupting
    - » Trouble waiting their turn or taking turns
    - » Impulsivity that leads to unsafe behaviors

- **Autism:** a developmental disability that is typically diagnosed around the age of two, when a child has not successfully achieved his language and communication milestones. While a lot of the literature states that many children who have autism do present with sensory processing issues, the severity of the issues can range from nonexistent to severe. SPD can stand alone, so it cannot be assumed that all children with sensory issues will also have autism. Symptoms of autism include the following:
    - » Abnormal social skills related to language that affect conversation skills and social interactions
    - » Lack of eye contact, appropriate body language, and other nonverbal communication skills
    - » Poor ability to relate to others and make friends
    - » Repetitive motor behaviors, such as lining up toys or inappropriately repeating what is said (echolalia)
    - » Persistent struggles with routines and transitions, inflexibility, and insisting on sameness
    - » Preoccupation with or attachment to toys and other objects
    - » Hyper- (more than normal) or hypo- (less than normal) responsiveness to sensory input that results in inappropriate pain tolerance
    - » Significant interest in seeking or avoiding sensory input through lights, sounds, smells, and/or touch

- **Developmental delay:** typified by struggling to meet developmental milestones on time at the same rate as a child's peers. For example, many children usually learn to walk around ten to twelve months of age. By the age of one year, many children are able to speak a handful of words or imitate animal sounds. Typical development occurs in a natural progression, with skills that build on each other. Children are often diagnosed with developmental delays shortly after birth or in early childhood when parents, teachers, and/or doctors notice they are not achieving their developmental milestones. Many doctors screen for developmental delays as part of their regular medical care during routine office visits. Signs of a developmental delay include the following:
    - » Struggling with the ability to problem solve (also known as cognition)
    - » Language skills, both expressive (talking) and receptive (listening and understanding), behind those of their same-age peers
    - » Delayed social-emotional skills that cause challenges with socially connecting with peers through sharing and turn taking
    - » Gross-motor skills used for crawling, walking, running, jumping, climbing, and skipping below the level of same-age peers
    - » Fine-motor skills, such as those needed to hold a pencil or use an eating utensil, are delayed, as is the ability to use both hands at the same time to build block towers, color, string beads, cut with scissors, and complete puzzles
    - » Self-care skills for putting on and taking off clothing, washing hands, eating with utensils, potty training, and sleeping are behind those of same-age peers

- **Down syndrome:** a genetic disorder that is diagnosed in utero or shortly after birth. Individuals with Down syndrome (also known as Trisomy 21) have an extra twenty-first chromosome. Some children with Down syndrome may be predisposed to autism and exhibit other sensory issues related to hypersensitivity around foods and play textures. Many children with Down syndrome have sensory processing issues that manifest in difficulty with motor planning, knowing where their body is in space, and tactile and oral sensory aversions. Symptoms of Down syndrome include the following:

  » Physical features such as a small head, short neck, protruding tongue, upward slanting eyes, unusually shaped or small ears, low muscle tone, excessive flexibility, short fingers, small hands and feet, and short stature

  » Medical issues that can include heart defects, gastrointestinal issues, spinal problems, sleep apnea, obesity, spinal issues, and hearing and vision issues

  » Intellectual disabilities that affect learning and acquisition of other developmental milestones for motor skills and language

- **Prematurity:** occurs when a baby is born alive before thirty-seven weeks' gestation. (A full-term pregnancy lasts between thirty-nine and forty weeks' gestation.) When a baby is developing in the womb, the central nervous system, organs, and sensory functions develop at different stages. If a child is born too early, some systems, organs, and senses may not have had time to effectively develop, so these children often have medical issues and are at risk for developmental delays and sensory processing issues. Sensory issues related to prematurity often include the following:
    - Trouble self-calming when upset
    - Issues controlling breathing and body temperature
    - Motor-skill delays in developing head control and bringing the hands together at midline to play and hold toys
    - Delayed social skills for smiling
    - Delayed language skills related to babbling
    - Sensory reactions to the environment with stimulation from nursery lights and sounds
    - Dislike of being touched or swaddled
    - Decreased organization and state regulation to breast- and bottle-feed successfully
    - Fear of movement, including dislike of being rocked or placed in an infant swing

Physicians and pediatricians are becoming increasingly aware of sensory processing issues. Many parents choose to discuss these difficulties with their primary-care providers at regular checkups, and this is often a very important first step in the referral process. Families who choose to use their medical insurance to pay for occupational therapy will often need to secure a referral from their doctor so services can be medically justified.

All US states have federally mandated early intervention programs, typically for children under the age of three. These therapy services are provided with a parent or caregiver present in their own home or in a community setting such as a playground or a day-care center. Many babies who are born prematurely are referred for early intervention services upon discharge from the hospital. Other children who have environmental risk factors, such as being in foster care, may be automatically referred when they enter social services as well. There are other medical conditions and risk factors, such as a developmental delay or disability, that may also warrant early intervention services for children. In addition, parents can self-refer their children for services if they have concerns. Sometimes, after a routine visit, a pediatrician may recommend referral to early intervention services too.

Occupational therapists are part of a team of professionals in early intervention programs nationwide. Teams can include special educators, physical therapists, speech-language pathologists, music therapists, nutritionists, and applied behavior analysis (ABA) providers, who provide intensive services to children with autism. Many of these programs are able to bill private insurance or are covered through Medicaid, but coverage depends on the rules of the state the family resides in. At the age of two and a half, children who are eligible will transition from early intervention to the public school system, with services governed by the Individuals with Disabilities Education Act (IDEA). However, each child's needs are unique, and the family will have to go through evaluations and discussions with the school system to determine whether the child is eligible to receive services after the age of three.

Current US Laws and Their Effects on Children with SPD

As mentioned earlier in this chapter, early childhood educators do not diagnose children with sensory issues or SPD. Instead, they observe children and share that information with families. Families then can use that information to inform their decisions, such as meeting with their pediatrician or family doctor to discuss what the teacher has observed. To support families, it is helpful for early childhood educators to understand how current laws affect children with SPD and other sensory issues.

The Individuals with Disabilities Education Act

IDEA, passed in 1975, is a federal law that mandates free and appropriate public education to eligible children, ages three to twenty-one, with disabilities in the United States and ensures special education and related services to those children. Under IDEA, children can be evaluated for and receive special education services, so that they can learn to be as independent as possible. If their disability affects their education at school, they may be able to receive services such as speech therapy, occupational therapy, physical therapy, and counseling. Children are evaluated for the need for services every three years or until they are ready for discharge. Parents, teachers, and therapists are active participants in the special-education eligibility process at school and will need to agree on the child's disability. Children who are eligible for services will receive an Individualized Education Program (IEP), which documents the necessary supports and services for the child that are agreed upon by the school system and the parent.

For a child to be eligible for an IEP, a clear impact on the child's education when learning in a regular education environment must be established. For children who have challenges at school due to SPD, the primary disability is listed as "other health impairment," which includes ADHD and autism. If the sensory issues are affecting the child's acquisition of skills, such as language, gross-motor, or fine-motor, then the term *developmental delay* can be used as an eligible IDEA disability.

Under IDEA, the child may receive:

- specialized instruction by teachers;
- related services, such as physical therapy, occupational therapy, speech therapy, and counseling;
- accommodations or helpful strategies that allow the child to be successful in the classroom setting; and
- assistive technology or the use of a special communication device, laptop, desktop, or tablet to assist with the child's learning style.

IDEA is legally enforceable. Disagreements and disputes over education can happen, especially if the services agreed to in the IEP are not provided, which could result in legal action by the parent or the school district. In the event of a dispute, public school special education teachers will appear on behalf of the school district, so it is very important that they understand their role in the classroom as it relates to IDEA. There could be very expensive ramifications, including, for a teacher or therapist, loss of licensure if the designated school personnel are not following the guidelines documented in the child's IEP.

Section 504 of the Rehabilitation Act

Section 504 of the Rehabilitation Act of 1973 is a civil rights law that prevents discrimination against individuals with disabilities in settings that receive federal assistance. If a child has an identified disability, such as ADHD, autism, cerebral palsy, or muscular dystrophy, the public school is required by law to provide accommodations that help make the school building and curriculum accessible to the child. The list of accommodations is called a 504 plan. An IEP is a different document, but it also includes lists of accommodations. School districts vary in how they choose to implement a 504 plan or an IEP, but generally, a 504 plan does not include access to direct therapy services. This means an occupational therapist may provide suggestions and consultation on ways to make the environment and curriculum more accessible, but the OT would not work directly with the student, in or outside the classroom, individually or in a small-group setting. Instead, those direct services are considered for eligibility under an IEP. Students with sensory processing issues alone may not qualify for a 504 plan, depending upon how the district views their disability. However, a student with another identifiable diagnosis such as ADHD or autism would be included under a 504 plan, and sensory processing accommodations in the classroom and building could be provided.

Effects of IDEA and Section 504

Under IDEA, in the public school system, there are many children who are eligible to receive services for free. These children with identified needs may begin to transition from the community or the early childhood intervention program into a public-school preschool or early childhood program on their third birthday. The process usually begins when the child is two years and six months of age. Eligibility for an IEP is determined by the school system using testing and conversations with parents and any other team members, such as private day-care and preschool teachers. As part of eligibility for the IEP, an occupational therapy evaluation may be completed, especially if the child was already receiving some services or the parent has expressed specific concerns that would warrant an evaluation. Sometimes an occupational therapy evaluation is not completed as part of the initial testing process, but it can be added later on.

Once a child is determined to be eligible for an IEP, the team will discuss appropriate classroom placement, such as whether a child who was formerly in a regular day-care program should transition to a special-needs integrated preschool. Special-education preschool programs, depending upon the district's programming, can vary from half-day to full-day classrooms. The goal is for the child to attend the least restrictive environment possible, meaning that the child receives as few supports as needed to succeed. Most children attend an integrated program, which is a class that includes students who are typically functioning and serve as role models. Some children require a substantially separate classroom or program, which is usually a smaller class with a lot of adult support and no peer role models.

Depending upon the child's needs, an OT may provide consultation services by checking in with the teacher on a regular basis to help individualize the supports for the child's academic needs and to provide suggestions and accommodations on how the child can be more successful in the classroom. Some children may benefit from working directly with an occupational therapist one or more times per week for a period of time, usually around thirty minutes per session, either in their classroom or in another room in the school. This is a great option for children whose sensory processing issues are affecting their ability to focus and to learn new academic activities. This therapy is also provided at no cost to children who are eligible, and it can be an attractive service because it can be provided without out-of-pocket expenses for the family. However, many children exhibit varying degrees of sensory issues, which are exacerbated by certain environmental situations. Some children function well at home with less stimulation but struggle at school. Others thrive on the structure and routine of a small preschool program and can learn when their needs are met with good accommodations. Each situation is unique, and each district has its own programming and offerings that it believes are successful.

For children who are eligible in public school, they will have a formal, documented plan, with goals, objectives, and accommodations on either a 504 plan or an IEP. (See chapter 6 for examples of specific accommodations.) Their eligibility is determined for a period of time, usually three years, with reviews occurring with the team members at least once per year. However, children can be discharged from services at any time if they are making effective progress and demonstrating skills typical of their age range.

Eligibility for Occupational Therapy Outside the School Setting

Aside from school services, there are other options for children. Some children do not meet eligibility criteria for school-based services; help is available for them, but it is generally associated with more costs and fees. Health insurance plans may include access to pediatric occupational therapy services, and some children may be eligible for services through Medicaid. Medically based occupational therapy services may occur at a child's home, at a private day care, in a private community clinic, or in an outpatient hospital setting. Parents may bring children in for therapy one or two times per week for forty-five minutes to an hour and either pay for the session out of pocket or pay a co-pay for a predetermined number of approved visits. There are also many private therapy clinics in the community that offer drop-in visits during the day or after school. Depending on the state, some children can receive services in the home, depending on their insurance plan.

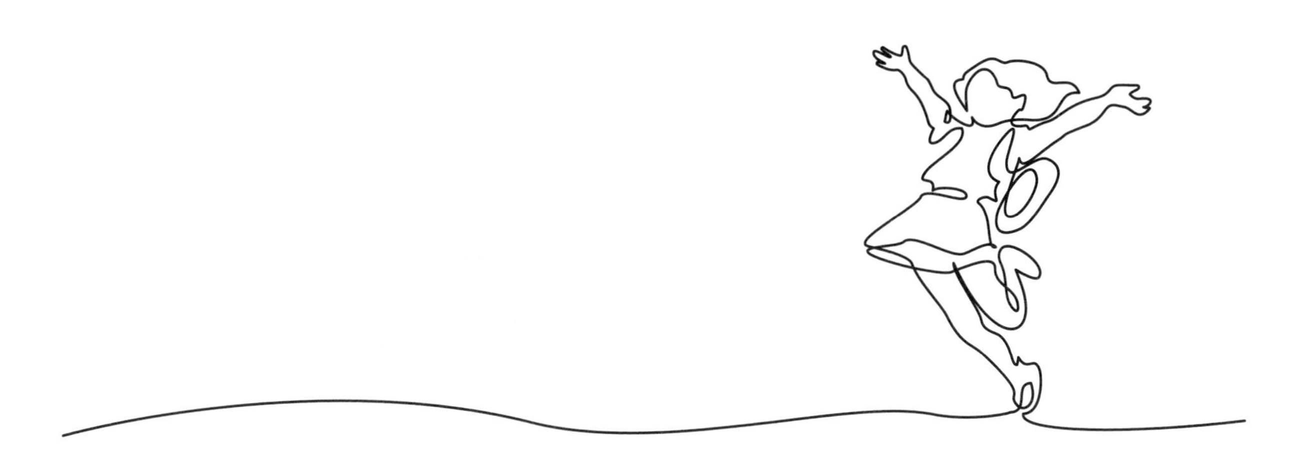

Many families choose to forgo using insurance altogether and pay a therapist privately. This gives flexibility for working parents who have children in early childhood centers and who might not otherwise be able to fit a clinic visit into their busy schedules. Some children do not meet the eligibility requirements of insurance programs, but parents are struggling at home and would like additional supports on how to improve their child's performance at home.

Whether therapy is through private pay or an insurance plan, service levels are based on the severity of the issues that the child is demonstrating. Therapists will use a combination of standardized testing, parent reporting, teacher reporting, and clinical observations of the child's performance to determine how frequently the child might need services. Typically, to be eligible for services, a child with sensory processing issues is demonstrating some type of delay in his motor skills. Children with significant sensory processing issues usually have difficulties with their gross-motor skills and core muscle strength for activities such as jumping and climbing. They usually have issues with fine-motor skills as well and are unable to hold a crayon or marker with the correct grasp. They might struggle with cutting with a pair of scissors and are usually challenged to complete activities of daily living such as manipulating clothing fasteners, remembering the sequences of getting dressed and undressed, using utensils to feed themselves, and potty training effectively.

Sensory Processing Disorder in the Early Childhood Classroom

The previous chapter discussed what sensory processing disorder is and how young children are evaluated for SPD. This chapter will explore what SPD looks like in the early childhood classroom and your role as an early childhood educator in the referral process.

Children Who Struggle in Early Childhood Settings with SPD

You are likely wondering about the challenging behaviors that children with sensory processing behaviors could exhibit in the early childhood classroom. Many teachers and administrators see these difficulties as behavioral challenges, but as you'll learn, there are specific reasons why children demonstrate these problematic but often uncontrollable behaviors. You may recognize many of these behaviors from the stories about Zion, Min-jun, and Ava. Here are some examples of the signs and symptoms children with SPD exhibit in the classroom:

- Demonstrate poor transitions from one activity to another or one part of the classroom to another, such as switching from free play to cleanup or from circle time to structured play
- Show an inability to sit at circle time in a small defined area for the duration of the session
- Bolt out of the room, fleeing from an activity or teacher
- Exhibit poor attention to or refuse to participate in nonpreferred activities, with an inability to "settle down" and get to work
- Are fidgety

- Seek movement, such as running, jumping, spinning, and climbing, throughout the classroom at inappropriate times
- Display an abnormal response to pain, either by not reacting to painful stimuli or overreacting to a slight bump
- Are forceful with toys and manipulatives, crashing and banging them together
- Avoid wet, sticky, or messy sensory mediums, such as playdough, paint, sand, rice, fingerpaints, dot markers, slime, and/or water
- Bite, suck, chew, mouth, or eat nonfood items, such as toys, markers, and clothes
- Exhibit impulsivity by moving quickly from one activity to another and having difficulty starting and finishing projects
- Show poor posture and core muscle strength that affects the ability to sit in a chair or upright on a carpet without fatigue
- Struggle with potty training and are unable to dress and undress themselves without adult help
- Cover their ears or complain about loud noises or unexpected sounds
- Exhibit frustration in the form of pushing, hitting, biting, kicking, or screaming
- Are unable to tolerate bright lights and frequently squint
- Are picky eaters
- Are very loud and noisy in play, hum frequently, and sometimes talk over others
- Exhibit poor motor planning or the inability to solve complex problems without help from an adult
- Have delayed fine-motor skills and struggle to hold a marker, cut with scissors, and/or manipulate fasteners such as zippers on coats or pants

Patricia Wilbarger, a well-known occupational therapist, made this important analogy at one of her conferences: "One bluebird does not make springtime." We are all sensory beings with sensory preferences. Just because a child has one symptom, behavior, or bad day in the classroom that also coincides with a symptom on a sensory checklist does not mean that this child is experiencing a debilitating sensory processing disorder.

For children who do have sensory processing issues, however, these struggles do not always get easier. Instead, they become increasingly more challenging and lead to intense meltdowns over time. Many children have tantrums more frequently and for longer periods. Their fuse can get shorter and shorter each time an incident happens, and they may react faster and with increasing intensity. Their personal safety and the safety of others is often compromised due to an inability to self-regulate or calm down once their fight-or-flight response has been triggered. The simple art of redirecting a child to another activity often leads to even more disruptive behaviors and is not always effective.

Some children in private early childhood situations who are struggling may be removed from the classroom, sometimes even sitting in the office of the director. Parents might be called to pick up their child due to inappropriate behavior or might be asked to participate in a conference to discuss the child's behavior in the classroom. Some children are even asked to leave their child-care facility because the school does not feel equipped to handle their behavior. In my professional experience, I have seen this happen more frequently in private child-care settings.

Too often caregivers and administrators see a child's "poor behavior" as the main problem, rather than look at how environmental factors can contribute to the child's behavior. Teachers and parents may think that the child is acting inappropriately to get attention; then, because the child exhibits some unsafe behaviors, she is asked to leave the school. While it's certainly possible that a child may act out to get attention, more often than not, children are overreacting to sensory input from the environment. Their sensory processing issues affect their participation and learning in the classroom, which manifests in what others perceive to be as bad behavior and noncompliance.

It's important to understand how sensory issues can affect a child in the classroom. It is also important to look beyond the behavior, to realize that the environment and the people and activities in it can play a significant role in a child's success or failure. Power struggles happen frequently with children who have sensory processing issues. Remember, their sensory needs are driving them to make choices that they think they need to survive. They are doing their best but are still learning, and they need the adults in their world to help them learn how to make better choices. Obviously, you do not want a child to continually make unsafe and inappropriate choices in the classroom setting, but you have the ability to choose how you will react.

Some children learn very quickly how to create and engage adults in power struggles. These struggles can become a focus and can be exhausting and overwhelming for a teacher. However, being calm, in control, and connected to the children in a positive way will help. Just make sure to have appropriate expectations and know when to compromise and modify the requirements of an activity to de-escalate negative behavior. This flexible approach is especially important for children in full-day preschool or day-care settings. When a child has been awakened early by a parent, brought to school, and asked to conform to rules and participate in challenging tasks for up to twelve hours, that child will struggle to regulate her sensory systems all day. Pick only the necessary battles, and try not to contribute to the intensity and frequency of outbursts or meltdowns.

Managing Undesirable Behavior, Tantrums, and Meltdowns

When a student with SPD begins to exhibit undesirable behavior in the classroom, it can be overwhelming. Children with SPD do not choose to misbehave. They are often trying to communicate through their actions that they are overstimulated from too much sensory input. How you choose to manage those situations can have an impact on whether the child's performance improves or escalates. Here are some things to keep in mind when you're trying to help a child through a difficult time.

- **Your own body awareness and tone:** Try not to overwhelm the child with too many words or yelling. Get on the child's level. Being too loud can make the behavior increase. Use a soft, calm, clear voice. Do not put yourself in a situation to get injured, should the child be prone to hitting or kicking, but squat down and be present. There's no need to demand eye contact, but be in a place where the child can see you and know you are there to help. Demanding eye contact or other behaviors to promote compliance in a meltdown can be another source of furthering the tantrum. Some children struggle with making eye contact, especially if they are frustrated. Some children are still in a place to hear you and understand, even if they aren't able to look you in the eyes. Encourage them to take deep breaths and help them calm down.
- **Use of touch:** Be mindful of your touch and using your hands on a child. Unless there is a significant safety issue such as a child unsafely bolting from the classroom, attempt to redirect the child by using distraction through your words and gesturing by pointing, instead of using your hands to pick the child up. For children with tactile sensory issues, touching them when they are overstimulated can cause even more frustration, leading to a longer tantrum.
- **Environmental stimulation:** Additional environmental stimulation can make it difficult for a child to self-regulate. During a meltdown, look for ways to reduce extra stimulation if at all possible. Is the noise too loud, with other children talking? Ask the students to use whisper voices, if possible. Is the classroom too bright? Close the shades or turn off the lights. Consider playing soft, quiet music to help eliminate background noise and promote a calmer environment.

- **A safe, quiet place:** Remember that cozy corner? If a child is having a meltdown, try to redirect her to a safe place, such as the cozy corner. Sometimes the child just needs a minute to cope and use strategies such as a weighted item or fidget toy. Giving children a few minutes in a safe, quiet space to sort through their emotions can ultimately help them to self-regulate, reducing power struggles and promoting a return to classroom activities faster.

- **Showing empathy:** Children with sensory processing issues often want their needs and emotions to be validated. Learn how to show empathy by letting children know you hear them. Some children might scream. Others might say, "I'm mad!" You can respond softly with, "I understand you're mad because it's not your turn," or words that describe briefly whatever triggered the incident.

- **Time to process what happened:** When a child is in the heat of the moment from sensory overload, she is often so overwhelmed that she is unable to use her words to effectively communicate what is wrong. Many children need some time to process their emotions or the events that caused the meltdown. Also, many children with SPD demonstrate delays in their language skills, which do not allow them to describe their emotions clearly at young ages. Do not demand that young children talk. They may not truly understand what has transpired and won't until later in the day or even the next day. Be the model and reinforce appropriate behaviors. Use pictures and point to different emotions to help them. "You were mad that it was time to clean up." Allow the child to point to a picture of her emotion if she is not able to vocalize it.

- **Understanding ways to help:** When the child is calm, talk with her about what she likes that helps her feel better. Try to find out what might have caused her reaction; you may need to wait until later in the day or even the next day. Many children will surprise you with what they understand and the important information they are able to share about their feelings and situations. Some children take longer to process what happened than others, but respecting their words and feelings is important in building an effective relationship. In a public-school setting, seek other professionals, such as a psychologist or guidance counselor, who might be able to help offer additional words and actions to take with children who are prone to meltdowns.

Your Role in Getting Help for Children with SPD

It is important for teachers to learn to spot the signs and symptoms of SPD and to begin to make changes to the classroom environment that could help the child participate more in daily activities. To do this, teachers must become the best objective reporters possible by taking data and looking for patterns. If you suspect that a child is having sensory issues in the classroom, take note of the specifics of what she is struggling with and when she is having a hard time. This information is important for any therapist to know about during the evaluation and intervention process. Here are some recommended next steps.

Make Observations

Observe the student and take some notes with objective data of what you see happening in the classroom. Don't worry about the why; just write down what you saw, with as much detail as you are able. Try not to let the child notice that you are writing down notes about her. Even if the child can't read the notes, many children are hyperaware of what is going on in these types of situations. Take data on behaviors such as the following:

- Child continues playing and does not put toys away in the proper location during the clean-up song, even when reminded to do so
- Child screams and runs away from the table to the block corner when asked to play at the playdough center

- Child lifts her hands in the air when they are dirty from painting and waits for them to be wiped
- Child sits at circle time for one minute on her carpet square, then sits for five minutes on the teacher's lap
- Child chews on the end of a pencil at the writing center
- Child throws a tantrum for three minutes but is redirected when given a fidget toy in the cozy corner

Once you have some challenges written down, start looking for patterns. Collect data on the time of day, details of the activity, people interacting with the child, and subject matter involved. Does a particular activity consistently trigger the behavior? Does the behavior happen at a particular time of day? Does the behavior happen with a teacher or a student? Does it happen during transitions? What happens before the child reacts? This is the antecedent to the behavior.

> Ms. Kay has noticed that Armando has begun melting down right before outdoor time. This behavior is new; Armando didn't do this at the beginning of the year. Ms. Kay thinks about it and then has her "Aha!" moment: Armando doesn't like to be constricted by clothing. It is now October, and he needs to put on his coat, which is quite tight, before he goes out. Ms. Kay makes a note to herself to talk to Armando's dad when he picks Armando up to see if he has looser outerwear. She believes that will help with Armando's meltdowns.

As part of the evaluation process, provide families with information about classroom performance or barriers to success, so they can share it with the OT, doctor, and/or evaluation team. With information, parents can help make informed decisions and move forward with making the best choice possible for their child.

Consult with Colleagues

Share these concerns and your objective information, while respecting the family's privacy, with another teacher, a supervisor, an administrator, or the director. If you are in a public preschool setting, reach out to the occupational therapist for the district, program, or building. Have other teachers experienced this behavior with this child before? Do your teaching peers or administrators have some suggestions on how to proceed? Are there modifications and strategies you can put into place in the classroom that might make it easier for the child to be successful? Is there a protocol in place to make a referral? If there isn't an effective protocol available, help create a plan of action to design one. The child who is struggling today is not the first and definitely won't be the last. How you choose to take action is an important part of a family's journey in receiving the help a child needs to succeed.

Establish a Partnership with Families

While it's important to keep families and caregivers in the loop, resist the impulse to call a parent and ask lots of questions that imply blame. Even if you have the best of intentions, you need the family to be partners for the child to make progress. It's best to stay neutral and to focus on what you can do to help the child, rather than tell a parent what you believe the diagnosis or situation is. Parents need time to hear the information and think about what to do next. The path to a proper diagnosis is long, exhausting, stressful, and sometimes expensive if tests or therapies are not covered by insurance. Parents might be in denial about their child's struggles. Some children perform better at home where the environment is less chaotic and they have more flexibility and fewer demands, so it can be hard for families to understand why their child is struggling at school. Certainly call parents with safety issues, but try to remain objective in your discussion. Make comments such as "I've noticed that your child is having a hard time with transitions when it's time to clean up. Her attention span for things she doesn't like to do is short, and she gets easily frustrated when asked to do something she is not interested in. To help her through this, I'm letting her know when transitions are coming and giving her a timer to use to stay on task." Avoid making suggestions to parents about reaching out to their doctor to ask for a specific diagnosis or asking whether the child is medicated for her condition.

Parents worry about their children and want them to successfully follow the rules of the classroom. Many families are struggling to raise their children with sensory processing issues. They worry about their futures and want their children to grow into independent, successful students and adults. More often than not, parents of children with sensory issues face lots of documentation and lists of negative behaviors that have passed on from one teacher to another; even staff who were not witnesses to a particular event give them lengthy incident reports.

Creating a collaborative partnership with families is ideal. Even if the setting the child is currently in might not be the right match for her developmental level at that time and the child is struggling to learn, it's possible to create positive, working partnerships with parents. Consider using the following strategies focused on proactive solutions.

- **Communicate with families on a regular basis.** Consider sending a communication sheet home with the child that outlines—in a positive fashion—what happened during the child's day. Remember that written communication, whether through email or notes, can be saved by parents and used in legal circumstances or furnished as evidence in a special-education dispute.

  Be honest but objective and professional in your documentation and verbal discussions with parents. Share your concerns with directors and other administrative staff so others involved in the child's care can use a consistent approach.

  For those parents who might be relentlessly asking how their child's day went, make sure you are offering valuable feedback instead of negative comments. It's always a great idea to provide examples of what the child has successfully completed during the day, even if it is a very basic observation, such as the following:

  - Wow! Reggie really enjoyed the sand table today. He played there for five minutes next to a classmate making sandcastles.
  - Saoirse patiently waited her turn during circle time to share that her favorite food that starts with *M* is macaroni and cheese.
  - Offering Marco a cube chair to sit in at circle time really helped his participation. It was so exciting to see him perform all the actions to "The Wheels on the Bus" for the first time!

- **Understand early childhood development.** Many parents of children with sensory issues feel as if they are all alone on an island. Before you can really understand how to help children who are struggling, it's important to educate yourself on what typically developing early childhood developmental skills and expectations are. This knowledge makes it easier to identify the behaviors that are more extreme and intense that could require intervention or a different approach. Biting, kicking, hitting, and similar physical behaviors are extremely common in day care and preschool settings when children are frustrated, but children with sensory issues will engage in these behaviors more intensely and frequently than other children. While parents certainly need to know when accidents and safety issues occur, reserve your judgement. Always be respectful of the family's privacy, never sharing personal information about a student with another parent.

- **Be compassionate and empathetic when communicating with parents.** If you call a parent or send an email, always show empathy. Share the details of what happened in a fact-oriented, nonjudgmental way, and do not place blame on the parent or use an inappropriate tone that makes the parent feel embarrassed or ashamed. Staff make mistakes, and problems do not always get solved the best way the first time. Children with sensory issues test their limits and boundaries, but with structure, consistency, and empathy, their performance will often improve.

  When sharing a child's struggles, report on what happened and how it was handled, but also provide a few strategies for how you might want to handle the situation if it happens again. Share your concerns and offer a solution. For example, "Does she take good naps at home? I'm wondering if there is a special blanket you might send in with her or a quiet activity she'd like to do in the classroom during nap time, if falling asleep is a challenge for her."

- **Consider timing when communicating with families.** Send an email first to ask about scheduling a conversation at a time that is convenient for the parent. Let them know specifically what you want to talk about, such as the child's performance at circle time. Unless it is a significant safety issue, avoid spontaneously calling parents in the middle of their workday to discuss the situation. Many parents are taking care of other important business, and interrupting their day could have a negative effect on their responsibilities and employment. If possible, let them go home and get their child's side of the story before having a conversation. Taking some time to think about the situation will also provide you with some perspective on the severity of the issue.

  Actions speak louder than words, so while communication opportunities serve to build rapport and show your expertise, follow through on your suggestions in a timely manner and continue to offer feedback and follow up regularly. Work together with the family to make a difference, rather than pointing out the issues without providing a thoughtful solution.

- **Devise an action plan.** It's entirely possible that there will be situations that will continue to occur, which may result in some difficult conversations with parents about their child's participation and behavior. While it's important to share some strategies of what you as the teacher can do in the classroom to help make a difference, there is also a bigger picture to consider. Some children might need to ultimately transition to a more supportive placement, and a gentle nudge by you to get the process started in the right direction is needed. Keep in mind that parents do not ever really want to hear that their child is struggling, especially if there are repeated safety issues with other students or teachers. Suggest that, while you are consulting with other teachers and making changes to the routine and the classroom environment, the parents consider speaking with their pediatrician and other medical providers, such as an occupational therapist. With information from a medical provider, they can assess the situation in more detail and learn about additional supports and strategies to make the child's learning experience more successful. Even though you may have the best of intentions, refrain from telling parents you think their child has a specific diagnosis or telling stories of children you've seen in the past with the same difficulties.

There will be parents who do not follow through on your advice to consult with a medical professional. That's okay. By communicating with the family, you will plant the seed carefully, respectfully, and professionally. You can spend time learning about child development and doing your best to offer the student what he needs.

- **Get support for yourself.** Be mindful that as a parent it is very overwhelming to hear all about your child's weaknesses, so I suggest meeting with parents alongside a colleague. If you are in a private early childhood setting, find an administrator or another knowledgeable teacher in the building to meet with you and the parents, even if it is just for your own support. You can process through the meeting with the other adult and talk about what you thought went well and ways you could have handled the conversation differently. Also be aware that in the age of smartphones, it is possible that the meeting that you are participating in is being recorded without your knowledge. As long as you are professional, you should have nothing to worry about.

  If you are a teacher in the early childhood public-school setting, then reach out to an administrator to find out about the school's referral process for when a teacher has a concern about a child's academic performance. This can be a place to start involving other teachers and school personnel, who can complete observations, offer some simple strategies to try, and begin the documentation process for an evaluation.

- **Assist parents in the referral process.** Parents need allies. Not only do they need help for their child, they need emotional support too. As a teacher, your knowledge of the child is important for those who are called in to work with the family and determine ways to support the child. If a doctor or therapist is willing to communicate with you throughout the process, consult your administrators about it, and sign the necessary release forms. With a busy classroom schedule, it might be difficult to talk over the phone, so email is a great option. Just remember to be factual and professional without judgement, because that email can be forwarded and saved for future use. The parents may have checklists and forms that they need you to fill out, as well. Complete them in their entirety, and return them to the parents as quickly as possible.

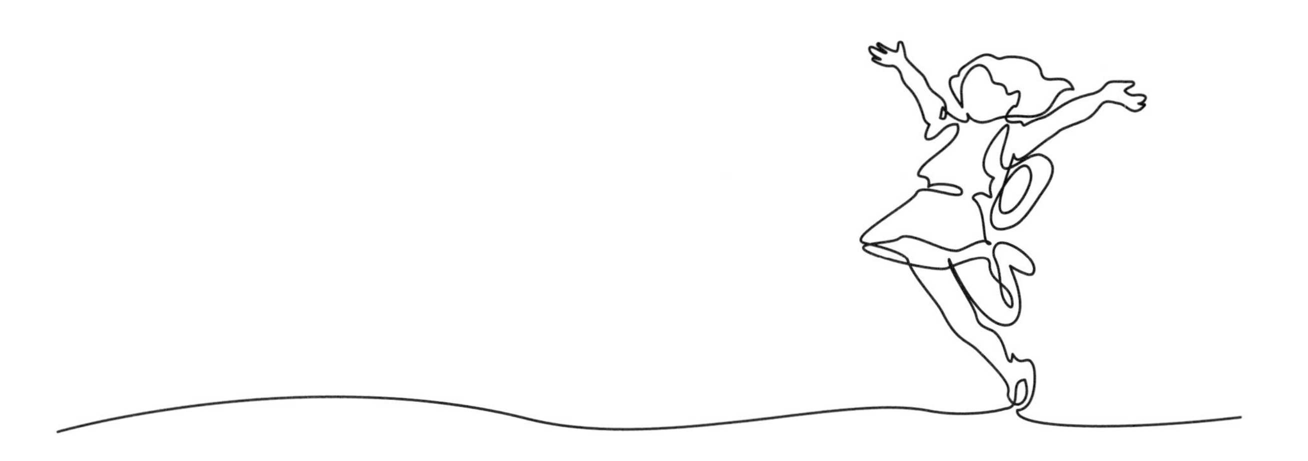

Once you have communicated with the parents about your concerns, and they have begun consulting with medical professionals, the parents may request a classroom observation by a therapist. Many therapists are willing to or might be required to complete an in-class observation of the child in the classroom as part of the evaluation. This occurs frequently for children in a private early childhood experience who might be undergoing an evaluation to determine eligibility for transitioning to a specialized public preschool program. Don't worry! The therapist's role is to watch the child during the classroom routine to see if she can identify whether the child has a disability that is affecting his ability to successfully participate with his peers. Just be yourself and conduct the classroom routine as usual, without offering the student too much extra support.

The evaluator will be looking at how the child sits at circle time. Does he use his language to communicate at circle or follow the routine to complete the body actions associated with the song you chose? While you read a book, can the child sit on his square and pay attention? How well does the child transition from circle time to centers? Does he go to all the centers in the rotation? How does the child interact with teachers and peers? Is he using language or actions to communicate or act out in the classroom? Is the academic content provided to the student age appropriate, or could it be that he's just not ready to participate in something so advanced, which is leading to participation challenges?

I wouldn't suggest planning all of the activities you know the child will struggle with, so evaluators can see an epic meltdown. Instead, let the child have a few moments to participate to his fullest, without intervening immediately as you might on a regular day. Should you need to support and redirect the student, how you do that and how the child responds will also provide a lot of information to the observer. Avoid stopping to talk to an evaluator during the typical classroom routine. Let the observer be a "fly on the wall" for a bit, then when there is a natural break in the routine, spend a few minutes conversing afterward to answer any interview questions. Or ask the evaluator if there is anything she would like you to engage the child in so she can get all the information she needs to help the child.

What Teachers Can Do to Help Children with Unwanted Behaviors

Think back to Ava, Zion, and Min-jun. These children are experiencing sensory processing issues in various ways in their current preschool environments. Their behaviors could easily be perceived by their teachers as challenging. While children with sensory processing issues exhibit similarities in their behavior, it is important to see these behaviors as symptoms rather than willful defiance or disruption. Even before a child has been identified as having SPD, there are some steps you can take to help the child be successful in the classroom. Here are other some common situations you might experience in an early childhood setting, with some possible solutions offered to help children with sensory processing issues succeed in those adverse scenarios.

> After several weeks of cold weather, there was an unexpectedly beautiful, warm day. After rest time, Ms. Carrie decided that having an impromptu snack time out on the playground would be a great way to spend the afternoon. Instead of washing hands in the bathroom, she grabbed a bottle of hand sanitizer and encouraged the children to put on their jackets, grab their snacks, and head out to the playground. She stood at the door to give each child a squirt of sanitizer in their hands on the way outside. Most of the children followed the directions, except for Kathryn, who chose to run and hide in the classroom under the table, crying and ultimately refusing to join her peers on the playground for snack.

Many children struggle with the demands and expectations of following a routine, so keeping classroom routines and expectations attainable and consistent are important. One small change in a routine can be frustrating for children who thrive on this consistency. It might be difficult in the moment to identify the trigger for Kathryn. Perhaps she doesn't like the way the sanitizer feels on her hands. Perhaps she doesn't like eating outside. It's possible that the simple change in routine is the problem for her. Whatever the trigger, know that as simple as it may seem to make a quick change in the schedule, not all students—especially those with sensory processing disorder—are flexible and adaptable, no matter how fun and exciting you think the change might be.

George loves playing with Kinetic Sand at the sensory table. He loves it so much that it's the only center activity that he ever chooses, and he often remains in that center for the duration of center time, ignoring the other academic activities—especially the less exciting ones related to counting and colors. Miss Diamond asks George to finish playing with the sand so he can transition to the math center in two minutes. She shares the expectation that once he counts ten blocks in the math center, he can return to the sensory center. George benefits from verbal reminders, so she offers him warnings of the transition. She then accompanies him to the math center and engages him in the counting activity. He's very focused and, for the first time ever, appropriately points to each block one at a time, showing great understanding of one-to-one correspondence. Miss Diamond considers asking George to repeat the counting activity, even though she told him he only needed to do it once. She wants to take a quick video to show his parents how well he did today. Instead, she chooses to give him a high five, tell him how proud she is that he counted with such confidence, and then sends him back to the sensory center.

Words and expectations are very important to children, especially when it comes to a nonpreferred activity. Mean what you say, and say what you mean, even if you gave the child an easier task than you originally intended to. If you accidentally set an inappropriate expectation that was too hard, modify it or change it to make it easier with your support and guidance. If the child succeeds in the activity or with the expectation that was originally set, absolutely offer her a lot of praise, to build a solid, trusting relationship. If Miss Diamond had stopped George and asked him to do the counting activity again, that would not have been in line with the initial expectation she had stated. A child with sensory issues like George would most likely get frustrated, and the situation could quickly lead to a meltdown that would affect the rest of his afternoon. Children with sensory processing difficulties thrive on trusting relationships, and the more consistent and reasonable you are with your expectations, while offering praise, the stronger your relationship with the child will be when it's time to increase the demands of the activity later on.

Mrs. Scofield has worked at this child-care center for a few years and has strong opinions about the types of activities the children should complete during center time. She declares, "These almost-five-year-olds absolutely need to show their academic readiness skills for kindergarten next year!"

Owen, who is just four, transitioned into Mrs. Scofield's class from another room a few weeks ago and is struggling to complete the activities. In the writing center, children are expected to write their names in lowercase letters. Instead of doing the work, Owen chooses to run around the class, dumping all the manipulatives from the shelves onto the floor and throwing the toys around. Mrs. Scofield is frustrated and calls his parent to tell her about his "bad" behavior.

Instead of seeing negative or bad behavior when children are experiencing sensory processing difficulties, educators need to look beyond the behavior to see the areas of need that are affecting how children react to what is happening each day. Make sure you have a solid understanding of child development and the curriculum. Children develop different skills at different rates; however, the process of how children develop their language, motor, self-help, and emotional skills has not changed. Unfortunately, curricula have changed to provide children with more challenging educational opportunities and expectations at earlier ages. Many children with sensory processing disorder do not handle these experiences well. As a teacher, if you have a solid understanding of the ages at

which children are generally able to perform certain tasks, such as remembering their letters, holding a pencil, writing their names, reading sight words, or sharing toys with peers, you will find it easier to spot children who are behind, to offer support as necessary, and to modify an activity to meet a child's needs. If you are encountering challenging classroom behavior, it's possible you could be asking a child to do something she isn't ready to do.

An activity in the four-year-old classroom is a worksheet that involves coloring autumn leaves, cutting them out, and gluing them as a scene onto a piece of construction paper. Noah is struggling to remain seated in his chair and instead prefers to stand at the table. He picks up his crayon, holds it with his fist, and quickly makes dark red marks across the paper, crossing over the lines. He puts scissors on his hand and cuts the leaves in half instead of cutting around the borders on the line. He then refuses to use a wooden craft stick to spread glue on the back of the leaves before pasting them to the paper; instead he walks away from the table and heads to the block corner.

Hanako sits on a seat cushion positioned on her chair, bouncing up and down while holding a crayon and coloring within the lines. She then awkwardly positions the scissors on her fingers but carefully attempts to cut the shapes, even though her cuts are choppy and inaccurate. Hanako sticks her fingers in the glue and uses them to paint the back of the paper before placing the leaves onto the construction paper. Both Noah and Hanako are struggling to cut, so Miss Cydne modifies the activity, offering them preschool scissors with small hinges to make it easier for them to cut the paper with accuracy.

Although both children are four years old, clearly they have differing skill levels and would benefit from slightly different strategies to improve their performance. As an early childhood educator, you probably learned quickly that every child is different. Likewise, SPD is not a one-size-fits-all situation. Noah prefers to stand at the table; Hanako prefers to bounce on a seat cushion. Noah won't use glue at all; Hanako has no issues sticking her fingers in the sticky substance to get the job done. Both

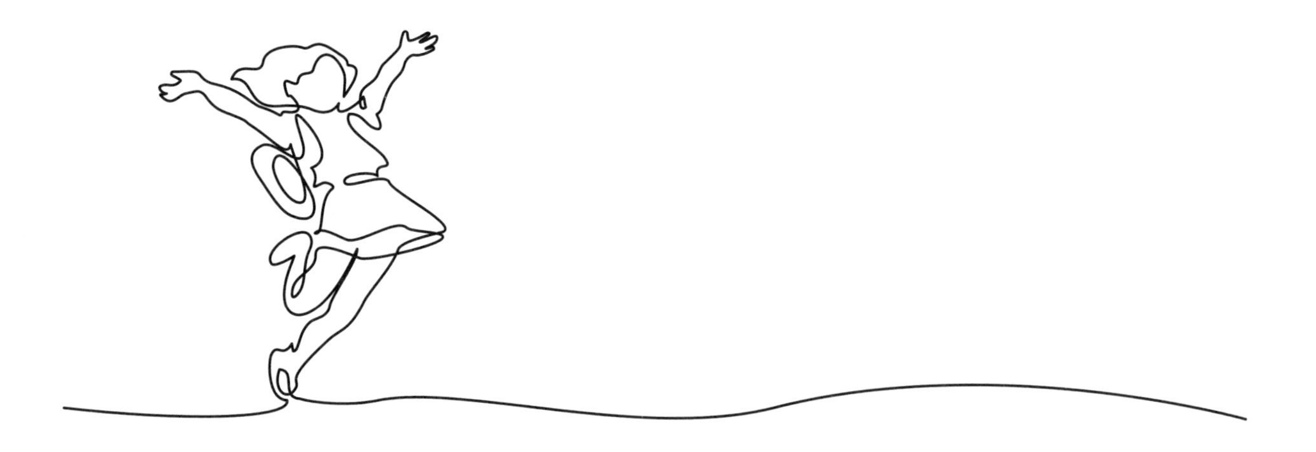

children are struggling to hold their scissors with the correct grip and to open and close their fingers. They need solutions that are unique to their own special circumstances. For example, Noah might benefit from using a glue stick instead of liquid glue.

What works for one student may not work for another. Early childhood teachers learn to develop a "bag of tricks," offering different options to their students, then observe the students' responses to see if their performance improves. However, don't make the mistake of giving up after one trial of a new strategy! Some children need multiple exposures to a new item before it is effective.

> The children are standing in line after going for a bathroom break. The expectation when standing in line is to keep their hands at their sides with a "bubble in their mouth," which essentially means "No talking." Derek is standing in his position at the front of the line, moving his fingers along the wall, feeling the divots and cracks in the paint. Derek fidgets a lot with his hands, but he uses his fidgeting to help himself pay attention and stay focused at times. His teacher, Mr. Thomas, considers telling him to keep his hands to himself and to stop touching the wall, but he refrains from doing so. The class waits for the last few stragglers, and then they head back to the classroom to listen to a new book on the circle-time rug.

Avoid power struggles with children and learn to modify the demand. Many children need to work through situations, but they will require a compromise, one that may not seem reasonable at first because the other children in the class may be capable of performing the same skill at a much higher level. Learn to "pick your battles" and ignore certain behaviors to build a trusting relationship with the students before increasing their work demands.

Is Derek meeting the expectation? No, technically he's not. Is he quietly maintaining his place in line? Yes. Upon returning to the classroom, the children might need to focus on hearing some new vocabulary words and learning prereading skills. Do you think this a battle worth picking? Is it worth frustrating Derek over this particular expectation when it might interfere with an upcoming important learning opportunity? In my opinion, in certain cases, it's better to let some things go rather than overwhelm a child with an expectation that could lead to a negative interaction and potentially affect the remainder of his day. Obviously, children need to learn the expectations of the classroom, but as the teacher, it's important to know that you do have a choice in deciding whether to intervene. All those little interventions over the course of a day could make the difference between an excellent day, a good day, or a terrible one.

Finally, if you're feeling a bit stressed yourself, be sure to ask for help from coteachers and administrators and take a break. Working with children with sensory processing issues is a challenge. Ask another teacher to cover your class for a few minutes so you can catch your breath and clear your mind.

Using a Sensory Diet to Help Children with SPD

Once testing has confirmed that a child is struggling with SPD, a sensory diet will be put in place as part of occupational therapy services and intervention. What exactly is a sensory diet? Many people are confused by the word *diet* and assume that it's related to food. The term *sensory diet* was conceived by Patricia Wilbarger, an occupational therapist well known for her work in sensory integration. A sensory diet includes all the ways we help children with SPD succeed in any environment they experience in their day-to-day lives. A child's occupational therapist will create a plan or routine for the child that's full of personalized activities, exercises, suggestions, and accommodations to help the child self-regulate or achieve a "just-right" state of mind. When children are organized, they are attentive and focused, not overwhelmed or overstimulated. Achieving this "just-right" state allows learning to happen, and it's important to find out how to accomplish this in the classroom setting so children can be at their best for learning.

A sensory diet aims to help the child function at her best and perform at an optimal level by being proactive, planning ahead for obstacles, and offering strategies for success. This approach is better than waiting until the child struggles to provide her own solution, when it might be too late after a meltdown has started. These strategies are shared with parents and teachers, because following through on them together in collaboration is important for the child's overall success.

A sensory diet isn't just one activity; it includes a series of activities offered throughout the day at certain times, from the moment a child wakes up until she goes to bed. Sensory diets are a dynamic process that can be flexible and adaptable depending upon the time of day and the activity.

Remember Zion? Here's an example of a sensory diet that might work for him. Since Zion is a sensory seeker, he craves sensory input through running, jumping, and crashing into other people. It's hard for him to sit down and attend because he struggles with self-regulation. Zion needs sensory input throughout his day that includes deep pressure and heavy work activities. He also requires accommodations, supports, and sensory items to improve his success. There is a lot of information in the sensory diet below, but notice that it includes a generalized, structured routine with lots of access to movement. It also provides accommodations and other strategies to keep Zion alert, while minimizing stressors. In addition, his parents are responsible for offering sensory input at home prior to going to school to get his arousal level ready for learning.

6:30 a.m. Wake up

6:45 a.m. Sensory input

Participate in sensory activities in the home prior to school to improve his self-regulation.

- Complete a short obstacle course for 10 minutes:
    1. Walk like a bear to the mini-trampoline.
    2. Jump on the mini-trampoline 10 times.
    3. Crawl through a tunnel.
    4. Stand up, run, and crash into a beanbag chair or a pillow pile made from couch cushions.
    5. Start again.
- Include transitional heavy work activity prior to getting dressed to help achieve a just-right state:
    1. Engage in a deep-pressure activity that involves rolling Zion up like a burrito in a blanket, having him sit on a parent's lap, and giving him big squeezes.
    2. Warn Zion that in one minute, after playing the burrito game, he will need to get dressed for school.

7:00 a.m. Get dressed

Use a visual picture schedule that shows the items Zion needs to put on. Allow him to put the items on in his preferred order. Consider using a compression shirt that he can wear under his T-shirt for deep pressure during the day.

7:30 a.m. Eat breakfast

Offer Zion the option to sit on a Movin' Sit cushion placed on his seat at the kitchen table; the cushion will offer movement to help keep his attention focused for meals. Or give him the option to stand and eat at the child's table. Offer thickened drinks in a straw cup at meals. Include preferred crunchy, chewy foods for sensory input as part of his meals.

8:00 a.m. Drive to school
His parents may consider providing Zion with fidget items to play with in the car on the way to school, or they may place a weighted blanket on his lap during the ride to help him remain calm.

8:30 a.m. Arrive at school
While he waits in line before heading to the classroom, allow Zion to sit in one of the cube chairs. Offer him a fidget to play with or a book to read, or give him a job to complete, such as putting the lunchboxes in the larger class bin. During the transition to the classroom, Zion might be best in the front of the line or holding a teacher's hand while walking down the hallway. Or let him roll the large bin of lunchboxes to the classroom. As an alternative to waiting in line, have the class meet on the playground until it's time for the unpacking routine.

8:45 a.m. Unpack
Zion and the other children place their backpacks in their cubbies and hang their coats up. Then, they sit on their carpet squares. Use visual picture strategies to help with sequencing. Remind Zion, "*First* put your items away. *Then* go sit on the carpet square."

9:00 a.m. Morning meeting
At circle time, offer Zion the choice of a carpet square or alternative seating such as a cube chair, rocking chair, or seat cushion to assist him in recognizing spatial boundaries and help him gain sensory input. Consider offering a weighted animal toy for him to hold in his lap when seated to improve his attention. Keep noise-cancelling headphones nearby as an option if he is upset and feels the noise is too loud. To improve participation, alternate sitting tasks, such as listening to a book, with motor activities, such as songs with motor movements: "Baby Shark," "The Wheels on the Bus," or "Going on a Bear Hunt."

9:30 a.m. Center activities
At the sensory table, include options such as playdough, sand, and water. Remember that Zion doesn't like getting his hands messy, so offer him a paintbrush with a long handle when painting, or offer him the option to wear gloves and a smock to keep his hands and clothes clean. Keep wipes nearby to wash his hands. Use a visual timer, such as a sand timer, to provide warnings to transition to another task. Zion may need adult assistance, with hands held, to choose a new center from a choice of two pictures, such as Blocks and Kitchen. Offer warnings at five minutes, three minutes, and one minute for cleanup prior to a bathroom break. Monitor any manipulatives he might put in his mouth for sensory exploration. Offer a chewable item to bite on instead of manipulatives.

10:30 a.m. Bathroom break
Place a sticky note over the automatic sensor on the toilet so it won't flush, and let Zion enter the bathroom first when there are fewer children, to reduce stimulation.

10:35 a.m. Motor break
Have the classroom assistant engage Zion in brain breaks, such as pretending to walk like a bear or penguin, hopping like a frog or bunny, or flying like a bird, to offer sensory input and reduce wait time.

10:45 a.m. Snack
Offer Zion preferential seating at the table, away from a lot of stimulation, near the end by the teacher. Zion prefers handwashing in a sink versus using sanitizer. Consider letting him use a Movin' Sit cushion on a chair when he is eating.

11:00 a.m. Outdoor play
Monitor Zion's play for safety. Encourage him to engage in play such as climbing and going down the slide. Offer transitional warnings prior to heading back into the building for lunch.

12:00 p.m. Lunch
Offer Zion preferential seating at the table, away from a lot of stimulation, near the end by the teacher. Zion prefers handwashing in sink versus using sanitizer. Consider letting him use a Movin' Sit cushion on his chair when eating.

12:20 p.m. Bathroom break
Place a sticky note over the automatic sensor on the toilet, and let Zion enter the bathroom first when there are fewer children, to reduce stimulation.

12:30–2:15 p.m. Nap time
Place Zion's cot in a quiet area, away from additional stimulation such as noise. Let him use deep pressure with a weighted blanket to help him fall asleep.

2:15 p.m. Bathroom break
Place a sticky note over the automatic sensor on the toilet, and let Zion enter the bathroom first when there are fewer children, to reduce stimulation.

2:20 p.m. Motor break
Have the classroom assistant engage Zion in brain breaks, such as pretending to walk like a bear or penguin, hopping like a frog or bunny, or flying like a bird, to offer sensory input, reduce wait time, and improve arousal level after rest time.

2:30 p.m. Snack
Offer Zion preferential seating at the table, away from a lot of stimulation, near the end by the teacher. Zion prefers handwashing in a sink versus using sanitizer.

3:00 p.m. Free play/computer play
Monitor Zion's peer relations, and model how to appropriately tap a peer to get their attention without pushing or shoving. Monitor manipulatives he might put in his mouth for sensory exploration. Offer a chewable item to place in his mouth instead of biting on manipulatives or his shirt. Offer fleece-headband-style headphones for him to wear when he's on the computer. Provide transitional warnings at five minutes, three minutes, and one minute.

3:45 p.m. Playground
Monitor Zion's play for safety, and encourage him to engage in play such as climbing and going down the slide. Offer transitional warnings prior to heading back into the building for pick up.

4:30 p.m. Pick up

5:00 p.m. Home for free play and/or screen time
If he chooses screen time, Zion may need a short motor break again before dinner to assist with his self-regulation in order to sit for the meal. Offer transitional warnings and a visual timer prior to dinnertime.

5:30 p.m. Dinner
Offer Zion the option of sitting on a Movin' Sit cushion placed on his seat at the kitchen table to offer movement to help his attention for the meal. Or let him stand and eat at the child's table. Offer thickened drinks in a straw cup at meals. Include preferred crunchy, chewy foods for sensory input in his meals. Include mostly preferred foods, with one nonpreferred food on his plate to explore.

6:15 p.m. Bathtime
Before Zion puts on his pajamas, give him a lotion massage after bathtime to assist with his transition for bed. Keep the environmental stimuli to a minimum, turn down the lights, and use quiet voices.

7:00 p.m. Bedtime
Cover Zion with a weighted blanket and read books in bed. Turning on a white noise machine or soft classical music may help with reducing stimulation so he can fall asleep.

How a Sensory Diet Works

We know that when a child's arousal system is in the right place, she can achieve a "just-right" state with her physical and emotional well-being. This means the child is in the right frame of mind to handle challenges and to be present for learning without overreaction, tantrums, and meltdowns due to stressors. As you can see in Zion's example, sensory diets are detailed routines, and they can be quite complicated and overwhelming for teachers at first too. Occupational therapists are trained to identify which sensory areas the child is struggling in, then to make these specific recommendations and accommodations to help the child perform at an optimal level. But as teachers, there is a responsibility to follow through on some of these activities. Collaborating with the child's OT and parents is very important, so that everyone can follow the same plan. Don't worry. Over time, it will get easier, and once you develop your bag of tricks and a basic understanding of how to use movement successfully in the classroom, you'll learn which kinds of activities have the desired effect you want for the student. You'll know, for example, which animal poses to try to offer heavy work, when to give a fidget toy or try a weighted blanket, or what to say to make that transition go a little smoother.

Many children who struggle with attention and learning due to being overwhelmed from sensory input are provided with a sensory diet that offers motor input multiple times per day for ten to twenty minutes. Motor exercises through the use of heavy work activities with a lot of pushing and pulling can help children feel more regulated. Notice how many opportunities there were within Zion's day that included movement. Some were for longer timeframes on the playground; others were short five- or ten-minute breaks to pretend to be an animal or engage in a "Baby Shark" dance party. There are so many opportunities to build in fun movement activities in the early childhood classroom!

A sensory diet is a dance that ebbs and flows and changes from one minute and day to the next. Parents, therapists, and teachers learn to know how the child reacts to certain input and plan to include experiences that positively affect a child's participation, while removing triggers that lead to meltdowns.

What if a child melts down anyway? Sensory diets are not simple, and sometimes the best of intentions can still lead to a tantrum or meltdown. One day the entire class is on task, and you've been able to complete three amazing songs and keep everyone focused on the story you're reading. Encouraged, you add in a totally new activity to make the circle time longer. All of a sudden, one student's behavior becomes challenging, and everything goes downhill fast. You offer a squishy fidget toy to help that child stay seated for just a minute longer, then make an executive decision to modify the activity to end it more quickly and transition back to the regular routine.

Sensory diets require thought, preparation, and thinking on your feet to know what a student needs to stay in that "just-right" state for learning and happiness. If something unexpected happens, learn from the mishap. Think about what happened before and after the activities, and take notes if you need to. Was coordinating a thirty-minute circle time effective with only one break, or would two or three breaks have been better? Is a twenty-minute circle time in the morning and another in the afternoon more appropriate? Reflecting on the activities, taking notes, and learning from mistakes will help you predict what schedule or routine works best for your current students and classroom environment.

Techniques Used by Occupational Therapists in Sensory Diets

Beyond the techniques that teachers and parents can use, you might hear about many interventions that occupational therapists employ as part of sensory diets. The Wilbarger Deep Pressure and Proprioceptive Technique (DPPT), created by Patricia Wilbarger, offers continuous deep pressure applied to the child's extremities and back using a surgical scrub brush. Some children may participate in this program with a parent and therapist as part of a home program, and as a teacher you may be asked to perform this technique. While it can be an effective intervention, it's a challenging one for teachers to complete confidently and consistently. I've had a lot of success with DPPT, but it's generally not something that a teacher is expected to perform in an early childhood school setting. If you are willing, able, and confident about learning it, then coordinate a session with the OT to learn more about it and see if it's a fit for your classroom and setting.

The Zones of Regulation is a classroom curriculum developed by Leah Kuypers, OTR/L MA, ED, that helps to teach children about their emotions and how to control them. Children learn to associate their emotions with different colors: green, yellow, red, and blue. The ultimate goal is to identify their feelings in the green zone, as being a "just-right" state of feeling focused, happy, and alert. The yellow zone equals feelings of frustration, anxiety, or silliness. The red zone requires immediate assistance because the child is feeling a strong emotion, such as rage, that makes him feel unsafe, angry, and out of control. The blue zone equals feelings such as sickness, sadness, or boredom.

Once children understand their feelings, this approach can help serve as a way to communicate their emotions in the classroom. Then, using a sensory diet, children and teachers can manage their emotions with certain activities to prevent overstimulation. *The Zones of Regulation* curriculum gives educators a common language to use with their students, as well as access to classroom strategies, so that even young children can learn how their energy level and choices affect their classroom success.

In addition to these approaches, public schools have Response to Intervention (RTI) programs. A child in the public school, whether identified as a student with a disability or not, can be referred to the RTI team. The team will make recommendations of what to do to help the child's achievement. If these strategies and their guidance do not improve the child's performance and success, they will suggest reaching out to a parent to start the process of an evaluation.

Setting Up a Sensory-Friendly Classroom

The classroom environment has a lot to do with how children feel. Too much visual or auditory stimulation can affect the participation of a child with sensory processing issues. Here are some important things to keep in mind in setting up a sensory-friendly classroom that meets the needs of the children and is not too overwhelming or overstimulating.

General Classroom Considerations

Many preschools use center-based learning. This means that there are sections of the classrooms used for different activities. Popular centers include an art center, a circle-time area, a cozy corner, a dramatic play area, a literacy center or book corner, a sensory table, a nature and science area, a block center, a computer center, a music area, and a fine-motor or manipulative center. To help children with sensory issues navigate the classroom, the centers should be organized and include the items necessary for the tasks.

The classroom itself should be free from too much clutter. Toys and materials should be kept in bins and on shelves. Labeling containers not only with words but also with matching pictures makes it easy for children to participate in cleanup. To reduce visual distractions and clutter, use sheets to cover materials when they are not in use. While charts and bulletin boards are a great touch, refrain from putting too much artwork or unnecessary visual information on the walls. Children with sensory issues can get overwhelmed by having too much to look at.

How to Create a Sensory-Friendly Environment

Early childhood classrooms are so much fun! Teachers spend countless hours designing bulletin boards; hanging alphabet, color, and number charts; rearranging the furniture; carefully selecting a library of great books; filling the sensory table; and finding fun manipulatives for children to play with. So, what does a sensory-friendly classroom environment include? All children, not just those with SPD, can benefit from having access to multisensory materials throughout their day to assist their participation and learning. Sensory-friendly classroom considerations help teachers find ways to appeal to a variety of children's sensory preferences through the use of fun materials that engage children's sight, hearing, touch, and movement. For example, there are different types of chairs that help children get their wiggles out while learning; weighted items such as stuffed animals and blankets, compression clothing, and tons of new textures for the sensory bin; and fun fidget toys that will add interest to the early childhood classroom.

Who Provides Classroom Sensory Items?

Sensory items to support students in the classroom can be costly. If accommodations for specific products and brand names are listed on an IEP, then it is the public school system's responsibility to purchase those exact items for the student to use. Should the team decide that using edibles or specific oral sensory items, such as a sport-top water bottle, are appropriate, accommodations can state that it is up to the parent to provide specific items. Unfortunately, private preschools are not required to offer specific items, but many parents are willing to purchase items and send them in with their child to use at school.

Classroom Furniture and Flexible Seating

Having the right kind of classroom furniture is important. Tables and chairs should be the proper height for students. When children are sitting in the chairs, their feet should rest firmly on the floor with the knees bent at a 90-degree angle. The table heights for children sitting in chairs should be about two fingers above the elbow. Consider altering the heights of tables, lowering some near the floor, so children can sit on pillows or on the floor or can kneel at the table. Raise some tables up to be standing desks.

Just having a variety of positioning items available can be great for the whole class, not just for children with sensory processing difficulties. Children have different learning styles and can benefit from a variety of flexible-seating options. Make sure to set firm limits and boundaries for the children in terms of how the seating can be used. Many children will realize how helpful different seating choices are and will usually comply with classroom rules regarding their use.

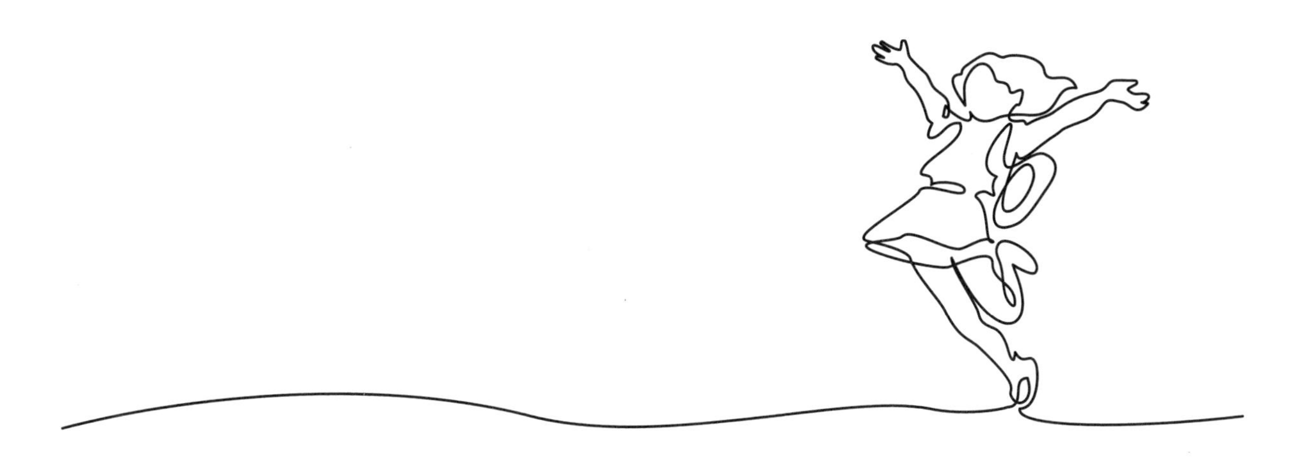

Many children struggle to sit on the floor for circle time. It is not uncommon for children with sensory issues to have decreased muscle strength, making it hard for them to sit on the floor and pay attention. Provide alternative seating or flexible-seating options to make circle time and learning more successful. Some flexible-seating options include the following:

- **Wiggle seat or Movin' Sit cushion:** In the Movin' Sit, the amount of air can be changed to meet the child's preferences. One side of the cushion might be bumpy; the other might be flat. Sitting on a disc like this can help children who like to move or who have a hard time sitting still participate with their friends on the rug.
- **Carpet square:** Carpet squares can help to define each child's space on the floor. Many children struggle with personal space and will sit too close to their classmates or have a hard time sitting still. Carpet squares provide a visual cue to help children maintain their boundaries. Some children like to use a carpet square because they can run their fingers along the pile, giving them an additional opportunity to help pay attention through tactile stimulation.
- **Chairs:** Some children can benefit from sitting in a classroom chair, rather than being on the floor. You can provide a variety of seating, such as cube chairs, rocking chairs, benches, and pillows. Peapods (an air-filled canoe) and beanbag chairs are ideal for children who crave a lot of support and comfort and would usually prefer to sit on their teacher's lap. For children who crave vestibular input, or movement, small rocking chairs, wooden-slat sensory chairs, scoop rockers, t-stools, and wobble chairs can give children the movement and input they crave, so they can focus during circle time.
- **Balls:** Therapy balls, exercise balls, and balance balls can be positioned on a sturdy pod for children who like to move and bounce.

Cozy Corner

Preschool classrooms should have a cozy corner, a small area that includes items to help children regroup if they are having a difficult time. Many teachers set up the book corner as a cozy corner. In addition to a few books to look at, they include a pop-up tent, teepee, or beanbag chair, along with a small box of fidget toys, a rainstick, or a weighted blanket. Sitting inside a tent helps to reduce visual stimulation, and a beanbag chair offers deep-pressure support. The cozy corner allows children a short break from the activity in the classroom.

Movement Corner

A movement corner in the classroom is a perfect example of how teachers can redirect children to movement in the classroom setting, giving them the activity they need without needing to make a special trip to the playground or use one-on-one support from a teacher. To show children what to do, post a laminated chart with pictures of exercises, animal walks, yoga poses, and Pilates activities. Children can choose three to five activities to complete in an obstacle course format. For example:

- 10 Jumping Jacks
- 5 Sit-ups
- 10 Frog jumps
- Downward dog pose for ten seconds
- Push the wall for ten seconds
- Rock yoga pose

To ease the transition back to seated tasks, use movement that involves the vestibular system, such as running, jumping, somersaulting, rolling, and performing jumping jacks, followed by deep pressure, heavy work activities such as slowly performing yoga poses, pushing against a wall, and doing wall sits. Do not necessarily focus on making sure children are performing the activities perfectly; encourage them to participate in tasks over a period of time. After guided participation and demonstration by a teacher, many children are able to go to the movement corner with a timer and complete these activities on their own.

Children who benefit from sensory input will often enjoy this strategy, and you'll be surprised at how independent they can be in getting their needs met successfully when they have the opportunity. Preschoolers are not always able to complete the exercises perfectly and in the exact number, but they understand the concepts. Giving children choices with the option of changing their routine helps to keep them on task and motivated.

Sensory Toys

Many tools and items can be used in a classroom setting to help children with sensory processing issues. These sensory toys may help give children the sensory input they need and improve their attention, focus, and participation. These toys are best used during free-choice times or as structured activities on a tabletop during center-based learning opportunities. Examples include the following:

- Magnetic construction toys and blocks, such as Magformers, Smart Max, Magnatiles, and Tegu blocks
- Pop pull tubes
- Playdough
- Sensory sand, such as Kinetic Sand
- Large cardboard and wooden blocks
- Foam puzzles
- Hammer toys
- Sensory playground balls with bumps
- Foam pegboards and pegs
- Plastic interlocking blocks, such as Lego Duplos and Mega Bloks
- Suction cup toys, such as Squigz
- Velcro fruit and veggie toys to "slice"

Weighted Items

When children are sitting at circle, sometimes they need more than just a seat to help with their participation. Weighted items are very popular and offer deep pressure and proprioceptive input to help children sustain their attention and focus. There are many different types of weighted items. Not all children have the same preference for the type of weight they benefit from, and these items vary in price points, which makes it easier for teachers to provide varying options on a budget. Consumers should pay attention to the manufacturer's suggestions when it comes to user height and weight recommendations. Consult with the student's parent or occupational therapist if you are considering weighted items that are worn, such as vests and blankets. Weighted items should have a wear schedule, which means that they are put on to complete a specific activity that challenges the child's attention, for a twenty-minute timeframe, then removed. Weighted items are not only beneficial for self-regulation when children are upset and need to regroup; they can also help children who are active and struggle to pay attention to improve their focus and attention to nonpreferred tasks. Use a weighted item, with a designed purpose, such as improving a child's attention at circle time or during a turn-taking game, or as a way to reduce frustration with challenging nonpreferred activities such as writing the letters in his name. Weighted items can help children engage in a task they are generally not fond of for a longer period of time with more accuracy.

There is a variety of weighted items to choose from, including the following:

- Blankets
- Lap pads
- Shoulder wraps and body shawls
- Sensory belts
- Stuffed animals and toys
- Backpacks

Weighted Blankets

Weighted blankets help to cover children up and can provide calming sensory input. These are great for children who struggle to fall asleep at bedtime or nap time or who need something to put on their lap if they are having a difficult time emotionally in the classroom. Weighted blankets can now be purchased in well-known big-box stores, such as Target or Bed Bath & Beyond. Online are many companies and individuals who sell custom blankets.

Many teachers and families try to construct their own weighted blankets to save money, but making a weighted blanket from scratch has its own challenges. It can be hard to evenly distribute the fillers (usually plastic pellets or fish-tank gravel). To make sure the weighted blanket complies with facility safety standards, it's probably best to purchase it from a reputable source. Most blankets purchased from stores are machine washable. Blankets are made from all sorts of fabrics, such as fleece, cotton, and flannel. Some blankets have one fabric on one side and a different fabric on the other.

Things to consider when using weighted blankets:

- Monitor children for safety.
- Make sure the weight is not too heavy and that the child can remove it easily.
- Never let a child sleep or lie under the blanket with his head covered.

- Not all fabrics work for all children, but most prefer soft cotton or fleece.
- The weight of the blanket should be about 10 percent of the child's body weight. An adult-size blanket might be a little too heavy for small or young children. Weighted blankets are a personal preference; some children want blankets that are slightly heavier than the standard equation.
- Get permission from parents before using wearable weighted items in the classroom.

Weighted Lap Pads

Weighted lap pads are like weighted blankets but smaller. This is a nice option to use for children who need something to help them stay seated for longer periods of time at circle time or when sitting at a table to complete an activity or nonpreferred task. Weighted lap pads are often a fraction of the price of weighted blankets, making them an economical choice. They are easy to transport, with fewer safety concerns than blankets.

Weighted Shoulder Wraps and Body Shawls

Neck and shoulder wraps are long, skinny, weighted wraps, almost like a scarf, which can be draped over the shoulders.

Weighted Sensory Belts

Weighted belts are clipped around the child's waist, offering deep pressure through the hips and waist.

Weighted Stuffed Animals and Toys

Weighted stuffed animals can be carried around as a transitional item from one place in the classroom to another. Children can hold them on their laps at circle time or cuddle with them in a cozy corner of the classroom to help self-regulate after a difficult emotional event.

Weighted Backpacks

Do-it-yourself weighted backpacks have been recommended by occupational therapists for decades. Children can wear a backpack filled with stuffed animals and heavy items for additional sensory input. Weighted backpacks should be used with caution, however: Make sure the backpack fits the child appropriately. Many children struggle with back pain from carrying around backpacks that are not fitted properly or are slung over one shoulder. Snugly fit the straps and securely fasten them. Compression vests, or pressure vests, may be a better option to provide deep pressure that is more evenly distributed.

Compression Vests

Compression vests (also known as pressure vests) are not weighted. They are made of stretchy fabrics, such as Lycra or neoprene, to create a form-fitting garment that feels like the wearer is getting a consistent hug. They offer deep-pressure input and are preferable to a weighted vest because they distribute the pressure more evenly, which helps with self-regulation. Like weighted vests, compression vests have a specific wear schedule of about twenty minutes. They should be used in conjunction with an activity in which a child might need some assistance to pay attention and focus, to sit and participate, or to aid in a transition. Consult with an occupational therapist when first using a compression vest to ensure it's being used appropriately and in the right situations. Parents may also appreciate knowing that an item such as a compression vest is being worn by their child.

Therabands or Fidget Bands

Therabands are flexible, stretchy bands that can be bought in different resistances. They can be tied around the legs of a desk or table so that, when a child places his feet on them, they offer sensory input to his feet. This strategy is often a good choice for children who fidget a lot and have issues remaining seated in their chair at a table or a desk for tabletop work. The use of bands should be monitored for safety in the classroom, because they could hurt if children use them inappropriately.

Tactile Sensory Mediums

Sensory tables and bins are a great addition to a classroom. Even though some children do not like to play with certain textures, for children who need help with self-regulation, tactile mediums can be a great way to help them calm down and improve their level of alertness to participate in a classroom setting. It used to be that sensory tables were filled with dry rice, dry kidney beans, or regular sand. Now there are many different types of sensory textures to explore. While sensory bins are usually used as part of a center-based learning activity, for children who struggle, consider keeping small containers of sensory items available, or consider opening up the sensory bin and redirecting a few children to it throughout the day to help keep their sensory systems from getting overstimulated.

Be watchful for children who could put items in their mouths for exploration. Make sure that any sensory items you provide are safe for children and nontoxic. For children who do not like messy or sticky substances, try engaging them in some motor activities such as a yoga or an exercise routine before you transition to the sensory table. Offer gloves to wear or tools such as shovels with long handles so children can scoop and play while they work on tolerating the input on their hands more over time. Do not overuse these sensory mediums. For children who don't like too much stimulation or are sensitive to tactile input, overuse can quickly lead to a meltdown or tantrum; keep the cozy corner and some calm activities ready as a backup plan. In the past, many teachers have utilized food items, such as dried beans and dried pasta, in sensory bins. However, given the high incidences of food allergies, teachers should confirm with their administrators whether food items are acceptable for use in a sensory bin in their early childhood environment. Here are some sensory-bin ideas:

- Play foam
- Styrofoam packing material
- Water
- Soapy water
- Sand
- Kinetic Sand
- Playdough
- Play dirt
- Slime
- Shredded paper
- Fake feathers
- Water beads
- Legos
- Manipulatives
- Shaving cream

Want to include even more sensory input in the sensory bins? Add tools such as plastic tweezers, tongs, scoopers, shovels, sifters, and bins and buckets.

Sound

Children with sensory issues relating to noise can easily become overstimulated in the classroom. Too many children talking, moving, and making sounds make it challenging to pay attention. You'll notice when a student is having difficulty with sound in the classroom. He might run to another part of the classroom away from the noise, or you might see him put his fingers in his ears or cover his ears with his hands to block out noise.

Be aware of noises in the classroom. Keep classroom chatter to a minimum, and control your voice and emotions so that your speech is not overbearing. Noise-cancelling headphones can help children participate in loud events or can reduce sound stimulation to help them pay attention to learning activities on their own. Many teachers are enthusiastic about helping but don't realize that using a loud, excited voice can actually lead to additional challenges and overstimulation. In addition, there are many great visuals for sounds that teachers can use to help children understand expectations on how loudly or softly they need to speak. (See Visual Voice Meters on p. 74 for additional information.)

Lighting

Lighting inside the classroom is important. Many children do not like fluorescent lighting, so consider modifying it by putting fire-retardant fabrics over the lights. Also consider adding softer lighting, such as table and floor lamps. Always make sure to speak with an administrator before making lighting changes in the classroom. While plenty of do-it-yourself options are available, they may not be safe for classroom use or may not be approved by the district or your employer. In addition, transitions from inside the building to the playground can cause children who are light sensitive to squint. Suggest that parents send in hats with brims or pairs of sunglasses to reduce visual sensitivity.

Fidgets

Many children fidget. They may fidget with their entire body by rocking back in their chairs, falling out of their chairs, or changing their body position, moving from standing to sitting to kneeling. Some children fidget with their hands by picking at paper, twirling pencils, or playing with their clothing. Other children put things in their mouths to chew on, such as pencils, erasers, marker caps, and clothing. Fidgeting is a sign that a child is trying to self-regulate.

Fidgeting can be used effectively in a classroom setting, as long as the items are safe and there are boundaries and rules. It is possible to redirect an inappropriate fidget. However, the new fidget must be more powerful to the child's sensory system than the one he has created or decided upon on his own. Remember, not all fidgets are created equal; they are a personal and individualized choice.

Just because you like a soft and slow squishy doesn't mean the same fidget is the only option for your students. We all have sensory preferences, and it's important to understand that children need options. Preferred fidgets might change over time or from one minute to the next. What worked yesterday may not be the best option for today. But when children are self-regulated, you should ultimately see less fidgeting altogether. If children are more stressed and anxious, fidgeting will increase. Don't dismiss fidgeting as bad behavior. With the appropriate access and expectations, fidget use is a powerful tool for learning.

Fidgets Children Can Use with Their Hands

A good fidget toy is an item that children can move or manipulate in their hands and that helps them pay attention and learn. Fidgets are not an option for all children, especially young children, because they want to use them to play. In the early childhood classroom, fidgets make great props for songs. Is your class singing "The Wheels on the Bus"? Hand out a toy bus to each child, and let them explore it while singing the song. Ready for "Itsy Bitsy Spider"? Colorful, furry, or sticky spiders could be a fun item to fidget with while you sing together. Older children who are learning more complicated concepts on the rug with their peers may benefit from squishy toys, fidget spinners, or other fidget items. Again, having an understanding of the rules of manipulatives is crucial for success. If children are using fidgets as a learning tool, great. If they are playing with them as toys and becoming distracted from the lesson, they may not be ready for use of a fidget toy, or the toy might not be the best option to help them sustain attention at that time. Popular hand fidgets include the following:

- Koosh balls
- Simpl Dimpl keychain toys
- Stress balls
- Slow-rise squishies
- Textured balls
- Fidget cubes
- Tangle toys
- Fidget spinners
- Therapy putty
- Dough with cookie cutters and extruders
- Slime
- Marble fidget toy
- Rubik's Cubes
- Snap and Click snakes
- Sequin toys and pillows
- Magnetic toys such as Magformers or Magnatiles
- Pop beads
- Slinky toys
- Stretchy fidgets
- Squigz

Oral Fidgets

Many children benefit from oral fidgets. These are items that are made for children who especially like to put objects in their mouths to self-regulate by biting and chewing. Food can also be used as an oral fidget, and chewing gum is a popular choice for older students. However, food can be a difficult choice in early childhood settings as there is a potential for choking and many students are prone to allergic reactions. Offering children safe alternatives for chewing helps channel their oral-seeking behaviors and reduces the need to chew other nonfood items that are unsafe, such as shirts, pencils, crayons, and toys. Popular oral fidgets include the following:

- Chewy tubes
- Chewable necklaces in the shapes of gems, sticks, or pendants
- Chewable bracelets
- Chewnoodles
- Chewable pencil toppers

Visual Fidgets

A visual fidget is something children can watch that might help calm them down when they are overstimulated. These fidgets usually involve bright colors with slow-moving liquids. Some children with sensory issues are fascinated by watching these items, especially when seated with them in a cozy corner. Visual fidgets include the following:

- Sensory bottles
- Liquid motion bubbler timers
- Bubbles

Practical Tools to Meet the Needs of All Children in the Classroom

In this chapter, you'll learn about practical tools and best practices that are particularly helpful not only for children with SPD but also for children without SPD. As an early childhood educator, you know how important circle time and center time can be for learning. However, many children need some additional strategies to help them successfully transition to and engage with classroom activities, especially nonpreferred ones. You'll learn about ways to include movement successfully in circle time, how to design visual boards that will support and motivate children to more happily persist through new tasks, and how to use timers and self-regulation meters to keep children focused and on task. Learn how to help children handle difficult transitions with ease, and explore a lengthy list of fun classroom roles children will enjoy helping with. Here you will learn those unique "tricks of the trade" to help make your classroom a fun, collaborative learning space for everyone.

Successfully Using Movement during Circle Time

Whether you call it "morning meeting," "large-group time," or "circle time," gathering the whole group together is an important aspect of most early childhood classrooms. It's a time filled with songs, books, and learning opportunities. It's often one of the first places teachers begin to identify children who are struggling with sensory processing issues, because while it can be a great place for learning, circle time can be a huge source of stress for children who have difficulty with transitions, attention, and performing in a group setting. If circle time is structured appropriately, it can also be a fun way to provide movement opportunities, meeting the needs of children who benefit from a sensory diet. Obviously, teaching a large group of excited preschoolers to perform the same activity at the same time isn't easy, especially when there are a few children who are struggling to get the routine down. All sorts of unexpected things can happen.

First things first. In the early childhood environment, it is important to monitor the amount of time children are asked to sit. In my opinion, for typically developing children, a fifteen- to twenty-minute circle time is ideal. When teachers have a solid circle-time plan each day, share developmentally appropriate academic information, and use movement breaks adequately, whole-group instruction doesn't have to be long. Consider starting with two or three activities, such as songs that have hand and body motions that give the children the opportunity to move all their muscles and joints, for example, "We're Going on a Bear Hunt," "The Wheels on the Bus," "Tootie Ta" by Dr. Jean, "The Hokey Pokey," "Macarena," "Head, Shoulders, Knees, and Toes," "Baby Bumblebee," "If You're Happy and You Know It," "Itsy Bitsy Spider," "Twinkle, Twinkle, Little Star," "Row, Row, Row Your Boat," and "Old McDonald Had a Farm." Then follow that up with an important academic learning activity, such as talking about a letter sound and looking for items in the room that begin with that sound. Children have short attention spans, so break up sitting time with movement opportunities.

Now let's consider what will happen when adding children with sensory processing issues to the circle-time group. The transition to circle time can be challenging for those who do not want to stop what they are doing. Circle time is also a language-rich opportunity. Children who struggle with feeling overwhelmed and using their language to communicate do not always perceive all this togetherness as fun. Plan to start circle time with a lot of movement right away. Some children might even need to spend a few minutes getting their energy out before the transition to circle time.

When Circle Time Doesn't Go As Planned

Circle time can get derailed quickly, leading to tantrums and meltdowns, especially when some children perceive it to be boring or "work." Plan ahead with more options and activities than you might need. Bring any supplies required to the meeting space ahead of time, preferably in a closed container or placed in a bin on a shelf that is covered by a sheet to reduce visual distractions. Otherwise, be prepared for it to get chaotic fast! Little children are learning how to wait, so making a last-minute song change and being unable to find the props is an open invitation for some children to leave their carpet square or start inappropriately engaging with the child sitting next to them.

Sometimes circle time just doesn't work the way you designed it. It's okay to make an adjustment to move on to the next activity. You can always modify the classroom schedule to do another, shorter circle time later in the day or offer a brain break instead. Make sure to take time to reflect about what happened and determine what you might have been able to do differently to provide a better learning experience.

Classroom Brain Breaks

Brain breaks are short five-minute opportunities in which teachers offer a movement activity. For children who need movement to self-regulate, exercises that allow them to move their arms and legs, as well as activate their vestibular systems, can be powerful ways to get them focused. Try activities that let children change body positions and require them to move their heads through inversion, such as completing a forward roll or touching their toes and reaching to the sky. Just a few minutes is all you need for a whole-class brain break. Find ways to sprinkle them into the routine throughout the day, but schedule them carefully. While I would suggest using them right before teaching challenging content, it might not be the best idea to do this type of activity immediately before you ask children to get their mats to take a nap.

These examples can also be used during whole-group circle times. Want more ideas? Head to the internet or Pinterest and search for "movement breaks" or "brain breaks for toddlers or preschoolers," and you'll find hundreds of choices. Here are some of my favorites to get you started:

- Throw a five-minute classroom dance party.
- Design classroom obstacle courses, such as jumping from one carpet square to another, crawling through a tunnel, or walking over "river stones."
- Create obstacle courses in the hallway to use for a transition to another classroom.
- Sustain yoga poses such as downward dog, cat, cow, upward dog, chair, tree, and rock for ten to fifteen seconds each.
- Create exercise routines, such as push-ups, sit-ups, planks, jumping jacks, hopping on one foot, and jumping up and down.

- Encourage rocket-ship jumps: squat down, bounce up and down to the count of ten, then blast off by jumping into the air.
- Pretend to be animals: stomp like dinosaurs, fly like butterflies, walk like bears, slither like snakes, crab walk, hop like frogs, donkey kick, or bunny hop.

Helping Children with Transitions

Many children with sensory processing issues struggle with transitions, whether they are transitioning from one activity to another or from one room to another, because they do not like change and are unclear about what to expect. When children with SPD sense a transition is around the corner, it's common to see their energy levels escalate, resulting in unwanted behaviors such as crying, fleeing, or aggression and sometimes leading to a domino effect among the other children in the room. While challenges with transitions are a hallmark for children with SPD, many preschool children without sensory issues also have issues with transitions. I recommend that you offer several different supports to help children complete transitions successfully. Verbal reminders, along with visual supports, can give children information on what to expect and how to move from one activity to another with less fuss and disruption.

Verbal Reminders

Verbal reminders warning children of upcoming changes are important. Often, children can become so immersed in their play that they forget that snack or outdoor time is coming up. Offer reminders such as, "Class, in five minutes we will clean up the toys. Then we will wash our hands and eat lunch." But sometimes just saying what's happening out loud isn't enough. Some children, especially those with sensory issues, do not process what they hear as strongly as what they see. To help children notice the reminder, flicker the lights as you give the verbal warning. Walk around the classroom to each group of children and show a picture of a child cleaning up, and remind them that a transition is coming soon.

Different children may need different reminders. Personalized "First _____, then ______," boards can help some children with transitions. For example, "Remember, Joey, first we clean up, then we wash hands and eat lunch." Other children might respond well to a sand timer. For example, "Sarah, when the sand runs out of the timer, it's time to clean up." Some children need a one-minute warning; others need reminders every minute for ten minutes until the lights flicker to indicate it's time to transition.

Every child is unique, so you need options. Differentiating learning is not easy to do seamlessly without a lot of practice and trial and error, but having several different strategies that appeal to the learning preferences in the classroom can make the day go more smoothly.

Helping Children Learn Classroom Expectations and Routines

Visuals, a form of teaching through the use of pictures or videos, are important for children in the early childhood classroom. Many children who have sensory issues develop their understanding of words at a different pace than children without SPD and have issues coordinating all of their senses when a lot of information is provided to them all at once. As a result, they struggle to pay attention and follow routines. Even children who can generally process spoken information do not always process instructions accurately on the first try; this serves as a major source of frustration to some teachers. Visuals help children understand the routine ahead of time, stay focused on tasks, and keep on track to finish, and improve their confidence and offer a sense of accomplishment. When children understand expectations and routines, they are less likely to have tantrums or meltdowns because they see what's coming next. This can make a huge difference in the overall class mood and in children's productivity and independence.

There are many different types of visuals early childhood teachers can use to prepare for transitions. You might offer a child two pictures to choose from, such as centers she can transition to next or images of foods she can eat for snack or the next book you'll read during literacy.

Job Lists and Classroom Helper Lists

Many classrooms teach and promote independence and teamwork through self-help skills and jobs in the classroom. Jobs are very popular, and many children look forward to completing them every day. Pairing a child with the wrong job can happen, especially since children with sensory processing issues might not enjoy completing certain tasks. For example, cleaning the table with a wet wipe might not be a preferred job for a child who does not like to touch wet substances. Try to make sure the job list encompasses a variety of responsibilities for classroom help, but consider children's sensory issues as you assign tasks. Children with sensory processing issues who need sensory input through heavy work and deep pressure may enjoy classroom jobs.

At the early childhood level, it's important that the teacher is in control of the job. I don't recommend that you allow children to pick jobs randomly. Assign the jobs ahead of time, and let the children see the list when they enter the classroom. This way, you retain some control, especially if you have found that particular jobs cause meltdowns, frustration, and stress for certain students. Start with jobs you know a child can perform successfully, and as her participation in the classroom improves, ask her to do different jobs. Don't overwhelm children with SPD by asking them to do every job one by one.

Some children like predictability, and not every job needs to be done by every child. Pick a few they are confident about, and rotate through those. If you have plenty of fun jobs to choose from, it should take a bit of time for children to notice they haven't had an opportunity with certain tasks.

Here are some popular classroom jobs that have dual purposes. They help children feel included in a classroom activity and successful, but they also offer sensory input through movement that helps their overall self-regulation.

- **Office messenger:** goes with a teacher on a walk to deliver messages to another teacher, maybe even hopping or skipping through the halls along the way
- **Photocopy paper delivery:** lifts and carries reams of paper to the photocopier for the teacher
- **Line leader:** leads the line immediately behind the teacher to minimize bumping into other children—a stressor for children who do not like being touched by others; being the line caboose is an alternative
- **Lunchbox carrier:** carries or pulls the bin of lunchboxes to and from the lunchroom
- **Door opener:** stands in front of the door and holds it open for peers
- **Paper passer/collector:** passes out or collects papers for the teacher
- **Animal keeper:** helps care for the class pet. Some pets can be calming to students with sensory processing challenges, while other children may have trouble controlling their bodies to be around pets and using enough control to pet them carefully.
- **Mat helper:** puts down mats and cleans them up after nap time. This is a great source of heavy work.
- **Board eraser:** uses erasers to clean dry-erase boards and chalkboards
- **Sweeper:** uses a small dust pan and brush to clean up messes
- **Table cleaner:** uses a wet wipe to wash down table surfaces before and after snack and lunch times
- **Chair organizer:** takes chairs down from tables at the beginning of the day and lifts them back onto tables at the end of the day
- **Paper puncher:** uses the three-hole punch or stapler with supervision to punch papers for three-ring binders or to staple papers together before they are passed out to go home
- **Library helper:** rearranges and straightens the books on the bookshelf

Social Stories

A technique developed by Carol Gray, a teacher and consultant who worked with children with autism, social stories are effective tools for teaching classroom expectations and routines. A social story is a personalized story featuring the child experiencing real-life situations and is used to help children make transitions successfully, understand how to share toys with peers, learn how to engage in social skills on the playground, or learn self-help skills, such as how to follow the steps to go potty or to wash their hands.

Social stories have become increasingly popular over the years as digital media has made it easier to use photos and images to tell a personal story. You can use illustrations or real photos of the child completing the sequence, then write a story to go along with the images that outlines the expectations of what to do and how to do it, including strategies to navigate potential challenges or obstacles. Children love seeing themselves as the "star of the show." Social stories don't need to be elaborate; they include a few photos added to a slideshow template with some basic captions in the form of a story.

In this example, Ms. Hailey wants to teach Grant how to wash his hands. She shares this social story with him throughout the day whenever it is handwashing time. She also provides an extra copy to his parents so Grant can read it at home too.

> There's Grant and his teacher, Ms. Hailey. [photo of Grant and Ms. Hailey]
>
> Grant had a lot of fun playing in the sand at the sensory table today! The sand feels so good on his hands. Sensory play helps the engine in his body feel calm. [photo of Grant playing in the sensory table]
>
> Ms. Hailey says, "Grant, go wash your hands. It's time to clean up from the sand now. It's lunchtime!" [photo of Ms. Hailey talking]
>
> Grant walks to the sink and turns on the water. [photo of Grant standing at the sink]
>
> Don't forget the soap, Grant! [photo of Grant pushing the soap dispenser]
>
> Add a little water, then scrub those hands to make bubbles that wash the tops, the bottoms, and in between those fingers. [photo of Grant washing his hands]
>
> Now they are clean. Don't forget to turn off the water! [photo of Grant rinsing his hands]

"Uh-oh, I can't reach the paper towels!" Grant starts to cry. [photo of Grant reaching for the paper towels]

"Don't worry, Grant," Ms. Hailey says. "Just ask a teacher for help if you need it!" [photo of Ms. Hailey smiling]

Ms. Hailey gives Grant a new paper towel. [photo of Ms. Hailey handing Grant a paper towel]

Grant's hands are all clean and dry, so he can sit down at the table to eat lunch with friends. [photo of Grant at the lunch table]

Video Modeling

Video modeling is also a very effective strategy to teach children new skills and offer feedback regarding their behavior through the use of these powerful visual stories. Many children do not choose the correct behavior or words during tantrums and meltdowns, or they need to practice and repeat new skills many times to learn the complicated sequences. Video modeling is a great way to share expectations in a way that lets children learn and practice without frustration. Besides, in the digital age, many children love watching themselves on camera being successful!

With parental permission, record the student, or another student in the classroom, completing a task correctly. You can even video yourself completing the activity. Or take individual photos and drop them into iMovie or another video-editing app, then add text and auditory voice-over cues to create a video. Create short, simple videos, using a script if necessary, that demonstrate a skill or routine. Then let the students watch the videos on a regular basis as part of their routine to learn the sequences and expectations. That way, if they become frustrated, they have something to remind them of the steps to take that are more effective, rather than exhibiting negative behaviors toward teachers or other students. Preparing and watching the videos ahead of a task and during other parts of the day helps with skill generalization and learning. Create videos for skills and routines such as the following:

- How to sit at circle time
- What to do when the teacher says it's cleanup time
- How to stand in line with peers without getting mad
- How to wait patiently
- How to maintain appropriate body awareness with peers
- How to pack up my backpack
- How to put on my coat

- How to write my name
- How to cut with scissors
- How to ask for help when frustrated
- How to wash my hands
- How to perform an exercise routine to help self-regulation
- How to raise my hand when I have a question
- How to turn off the computer or tablet

Visual Schedule

To show the order of the classroom routine, place pictures in a chart in a vertical orientation, then remove each picture as the activity is completed. This approach will help reduce anxiety about what's coming next and help children see just how many things they'll need to do before their parents pick them up at the end of the day. Classroom routines outline the day, starting with unpacking their belongings, morning circle, snack, center times, restroom times, lunch, recess, nap time, free play, and cleanup. The actual time that each event occurs is not important to young children; they just want to know what comes next.

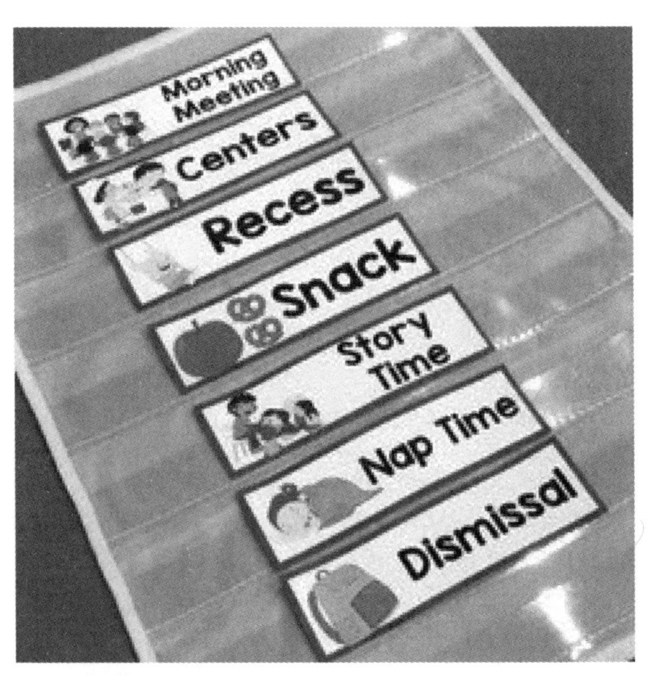

Source: © 2020 Vanessa Levin, The Teaching Tribe/Pre-K Pages. Used with permission.

Work Boards

Preschool settings with learning centers often have a large work board. This is an opportunity for children to see which centers are open and closed. When transitioning from circle time to centers, they can see what's available. Some centers allow only so many participants at one time, so if a center is full, children can choose a different one. Children place a personalized clip next to the photo of the center they want to attend. Some classes rotate through centers, depending on where they start. Others let children choose another center when a space is available, but the child is responsible for moving her clip and then heading to the correct center. Classroom work boards can be helpful to add structure and reduce chaos in the classroom with so many students engaging in different activities at the same time.

Personalized Work Charts

In addition to visual classroom routines, many children will need their own personalized routine charts with photos, to improve their participation in activities they don't like and to help them communicate when they are frustrated or overwhelmed. Sometimes the classroom work board is too much for children with sensory processing difficulties. They forget the expectations and impulsively make decisions to go to different centers. A personalized work chart uses the same pictures from the classroom work board with a clip, but it helps individual children move from one center to another more independently. Personalized work charts might be laminated strips with icons attached to them with Velcro. Some children like to remove the icon when they complete the task; others like to flip it over to indicate it's done, like their own personal to-do list.

First, Then Boards

A "First, Then" board is a great way to help children participate in tasks they find challenging or uninteresting. Many times teachers speak to children about the rules and expectations, but for children with language or processing delays in a busy classroom, it's hard to understand the expectation.

To create a First, Then board, take pictures of the activities present in the classroom. Then separate them into preferred and nonpreferred tasks. Generally, the child is asked to complete a nonpreferred activity first, followed by an activity she is motivated to engage in. To help a child understand how to use the First, Then board, begin with two highly preferred activities. Preferred and nonpreferred activities will vary from one child to another, and sometimes what was once preferred can quickly become nonpreferred. Having access to a generic board with a lot of pictures will give you the flexibility to customize a First, Then board to the individual needs of the child.

Many children, when given the choice, will choose nonchallenging work or simple activities they like in order to avoid learning tasks they find challenging. However, avoidance does not help them work through and experience all that a classroom has to offer. Not all children need First, Then boards, but they're a great strategy to include for children who are just beginning preschool and have difficulty transitioning from one activity to another and completing classroom expectations on their own. Here are some examples of ways to use a First, Then board:

- First play with trains (preferred), then you can choose blocks (preferred).
- First play with sand (preferred), then eat snack (preferred).
- First complete the puzzle (nonpreferred), then you can play in the sensory table (preferred).
- First write your name (nonpreferred), then go to the art center (preferred).
- First we'll sing "Old McDonald Had a Farm" (nonpreferred), then you can read books (preferred).
- First tell me your favorite color (nonpreferred), then you can play in the kitchen (preferred).

Token Boards

Token boards reward children for participating in nonpreferred activities. Sometimes they are used to help children stay on task and can be modified based on the child. Let's say you want your student to start, participate in, and complete a ten-piece puzzle. Each time the child does what is expected, she receives a sticker, check mark, or personalized picture to place in a grid. Maybe, for instance, she receives a token for every piece she puts into the puzzle, even if you need to cue her on the right spot. Then, when she fills up the grid with tokens, she earns a reward. Rewards will vary based on the child's interests and the difficulty of the task. Teachers then have flexibility to offer rewards that fit into the schedule and routine. Sometimes token boards are used in conjunction with First, Then boards: "First, finish the puzzle, then earn time coloring." Some children need rewards to get started, sustain their attention, and finish a task they don't prefer to do, but this can be a helpful strategy to give all children a little motivation.

Noise Meters

Noise meters are very helpful in a classroom setting where there are lots of children. Over time, children can just seem to get louder and louder and louder, to the point that it's hard to focus and nothing seems to get accomplished. When children with SPD are present, it's very important to keep the sound levels of the classroom controlled, because chaotic sounds and energy in a classroom can make it harder for these children to get through the day without incidences or meltdowns.

Noise meters assign an expectation of the child's voice to an activity. It can be hard for children to regulate or modulate the volume of their voices, but seeing a visual is a great way to help them remember to talk quietly or loudly, depending on the expectation. Noise meters can be illustrated in pictures, but there are app options available too. Noise meters can be used on a personal level for individual students, but they are an excellent tool the entire class can benefit from.

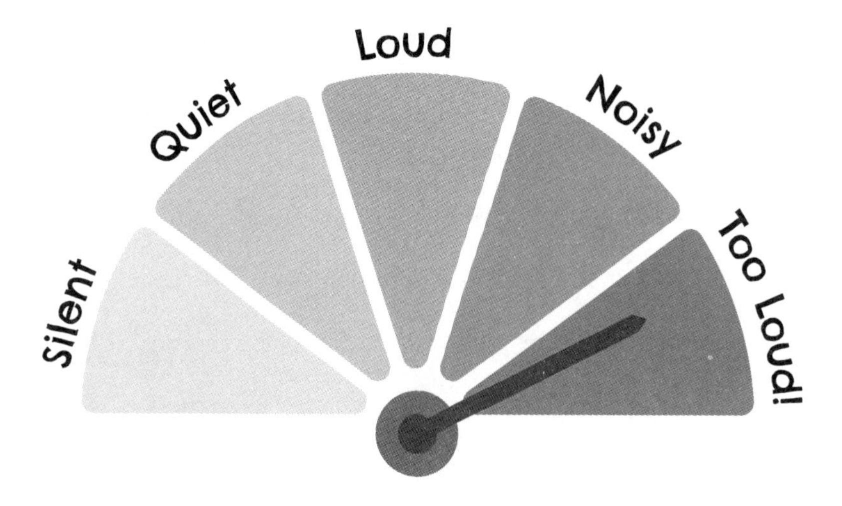

An easy one can be a vertical chart with a green bar at the bottom and the words "No voice." Next is a yellow bar with the word *whisper*. The third bar is orange, with the words "Classroom voice." At the top of the chart is a red bar with the words "Outdoor voice." You can place different meters at the different learning centers, with a clothespin or paper arrow pointing to the noise expectation for each center. For example, if a center is a no-talking center, the arrow would point to the green bar. In a center where quiet conversation is okay, the arrow would point to the yellow bar. Where it is okay to be a little louder, the arrow would point to the orange bar. If the children are getting too loud, point to the red bar, then point to the appropriate color to remind the children where their noise level should be.

Self-Regulation Meters

Self-regulation meters are important to use with children who have sensory issues. Similar to the concept of a noise meter, children use a picture to identify their energy level in varying degrees from low to high. Ideally they will identify their energy levels are "just right for learning." The goal for a child is to develop an understanding of her arousal and energy levels, so she can identify what type of sensory input can help her improve her level of alertness to pay attention or, conversely, reduce her stimulation level to calm down and focus. When children understand how to notice their alertness levels, they can make adjustments on their own and advocate for their needs rather than relying on a teacher to guide them. Many of these meters look like speedometers, with a plastic arrow that the child can use to point, to tell the teacher how she is feeling: "OK," "A little upset," "Frustrated," "Angry," "Meltdown." Alternatively, the meter can show energy: "Low," "Just right," "High."

When occupational therapists help children to learn about self-regulation, they often use a popular program called *The Alert Program*, created by occupational therapists Mary Sue Williams and Sherry Shellenberger. Through a variety of activities, children learn to relate their bodies to that of a car engine that has different gears to run slow, fast, or "just right." Then they can identify different activities they can use throughout the day to change their level of alertness appropriately to remain in control. Not all children identify with the car analogy; some might understand animals or personalized wording better. The *Zones of Regulation* program by Leah Kuypers, discussed earlier, also includes self-regulation visuals. Self-regulation meters are a visual way for a teacher to connect with a student to teach language that describes the child's emotional state and enables the student to show control and understanding of her body. This way, the child and teacher can work together to promote self-regulation. Here is an example of how a teacher might use a variety of visuals with a student to improve self-regulation.

> Ms. Kaitlin: Wow, Bella, you are really enjoying jumping today. Why don't you show me on the meter where your energy level is right now.
>
> Bella: (maneuvers the plastic needle to point to *High* and screams) Too high!

Ms. Kaitlin: Yes! I agree with you. I see you jumping up and down at the sensory center. Do you see the sand on the floor from your jumping while holding the container? The engine inside your body is moving fast. We need you to feel "just right." (offers Bella a laminated visual of classroom exercises that are part of Bella's sensory diet) Let's choose three exercises to do that will help you get ready to pay attention for circle time.

Bella reaches toward the chart and removes the pictures of bear-walking, rocket-ship jumps, and the downward-dog yoga pose. She reattaches them at the bottom to create a sequence. With a timer set for three minutes, she performs the exercises as Ms. Kaitlin watches. When the timer beeps, Ms. Kaitlin brings out the self-regulation meter again.

Ms. Kaitlin: Can you show me how you feel now?

Bella maneuvers the needle to point to "Just right."

Ms. Kaitlin: Yes, you are! Great job, Bella! I see that your body is calm and you are doing an excellent job listening to my directions.

She offers her hand for a high five and asks Bella to go have a seat on the carpet square for literacy time.

It's okay if the child does not automatically self-regulate. Have another discussion regarding what can be done, set the timer, and revisit the child's energy level after the strategy is complete. This approach is not always perfect; sometimes children can get overstimulated instead of self-regulating. But the key is having a way to communicate with each other to problem solve.

Timers

Timers are a great visual reminder too. There are digital timers, time timers, time trackers, kitchen timers, talking timers, sand timers, watch timers, and even apps that count down time. Children often have preferences for certain timers, so don't get frustrated if one doesn't work. The child might need a different one that works for her learning style. Children with auditory sensitivity generally don't like timers that make ticking noises or loud sounds. Many children with sensory issues benefit from visual timers, such as sand timers or colored timers that show how much time is left without numbers or sounds.

Making Pictures and Visuals

Visuals are an excellent way to help keep the classroom running smoothly, but creating them can be overwhelming. There are many resources that offer printable pictures that can be laminated and used to indicate areas of the classroom or where materials are stored. These pictures are an excellent way to help create visual classroom routines too. There are many sites where you can create your own; others charge a small fee for visuals that are already designed. Here are some popular options:

- **Boardmaker (https://goboardmaker.com/):** Boardmaker is a computer software program that includes access to more than 40,000 pictures and symbols that can be printed in black and white or color. It's available online, but many public schools purchase this software to use for speech therapy and classroom use. Ask your colleagues to see if it's available at your school.
- **LessonPix (https://lessonpix.com/):** For a few dollars per month, teachers can access thousands of clip-art images to customize and create classroom picture schedules, routines, work boards, token systems, certificates, stories, and books.
- **Pinterest (www.pinterest.com):** Pinterest allows users to search for inspiration by typing in keywords and then sharing the link or the photo on organized virtual boards. It leads you to websites where you can print visuals. Depending on the end source, visuals may be free or may require purchase through websites such as www.teacherspayteachers.com.

If you are skilled at using graphics or taking your own photos and you see something you like, but that doesn't quite work for your class as designed, use others' designs for inspiration. Create something that works as the best solution for your class. If any of the parents of the children in your class are handy or crafty, ask them to provide copies of any visuals the child is using at home or in therapy. Share visuals that are working well in the classroom with parents too.

Make sure you understand your employer's policy regarding taking photos of children. You must get permission and adhere to any parental preferences regarding the use of children's photos.

Technology Tools to Help Children with SPD

As discussed in the previous chapter, teachers can use technology, such as social stories and video modeling, to help children become more comfortable with the classroom routine. There are many other technology tools marketed to early childhood educators, as well as opinions about the role of technology in the early childhood classroom. This chapter will help you make sense of it all.

Children are exposed to technology through the use of tablets and smartphones. While there certainly needs to be a balance, numerous opportunities for use of technology in the classroom are available to help children with SPD improve their self-regulation and participation. Technology should not be the only option, but you can supplement educational experiences with activities, apps, and devices that have been carefully selected ahead of time. Many classrooms are now equipped with Smart boards, which are a great way to show the entire class fun videos that offer helpful exercise and brain breaks to get sensory input throughout the day.

Technology Dos and Don'ts in the Early Childhood Classroom

- Refer to the National Association for the Education of Young Children (NAEYC) position statement on technology and interactive media. This document offers information on best practices for sharing developmentally appropriate content with young children and effectively promoting digital citizenship through digital media in the classroom setting.
- Put any device in a protective case, and enable passcodes for security and safety purposes.
- You can find excellent content for classrooms online on YouTube.com and other internet websites. Before you show anything to the children, view the content to make sure it's appropriate for your intended audience.
- Speak with your curriculum providers and administrators, and understand your facility's technology policy. If you are allowed to share images online, make sure you have a signed parental release form for each child.
- Do not rely on technology to replace you, but use digital tools to supplement lesson plans and make learning easier and more interactive for a variety of learning styles.
- Monitor the amount of time technology is used in your classroom. Children get so much time on tablets and devices outside of school, good old-fashioned playtime at the sensory table, in the block center, or climbing and running on the playground should be the first priority.
- Make sure children are getting equal access. With the benefit of technology also comes the possibility that some children will struggle with the transition away from the device when the activity is over. Set rules and limits on access, and enforce them. For example, let each child have an opportunity to turn one page during the interactive e-book session. Use timers, token boards, and clear visuals to provide expectations on technology use.
- Use transitional warnings with technology, reminding students that the tablet will be put away in a few minutes. Model appropriate use of the device yourself by setting a timer, then modeling how to close down and transition away from the device without frustration.

- After an activity using a device, plan a highly motivating activity, such as a brain break or sensory-table play, to assist children with transitioning away from the digital tool.

Tablets and Smartphones

There are many uses for tablets and smartphones in a classroom. While it is certainly important to offer children manipulatives and more traditional learning opportunities, for children with sensory processing issues, having access to a device offers opportunities for multisensory learning activities or supplemental activities to support academic tasks.

> Ricardo had a hard time listening to the book ***The Day the Crayons Quit*** at circle time when it was read aloud by his teacher. However, when Ms. Kay read it to him from her tablet, and Ricardo was able to witness a more exciting rendition of the book with animations and music, and he had a turn to swipe through the pages, he happily engaged with his peers during literacy time without any frustration.

Whether the device is used to explore interactive e-books, as a way to play music for motor breaks, as a timer to warn a student of an upcoming transition, or as a reward for a student who successfully completes a nonpreferred activity, there are benefits of using a tablet in the classroom. Many children like using their tablet as part of a reward system. Did they work hard on keeping their composure for something that is generally a major challenge? While it wouldn't be the first type of reward to offer, you may want to consider asking parents if rewarding their child with time on a tablet for a few minutes is something they would agree with.

The most ubiquitous tablets and smartphones are iPads and iPhones. Android tablets are different from iPads. They are generally less expensive, and popular toy companies such as VTech and LeapFrog make child-friendly learning tablets with educational games that include parental controls. Android tablets can be loaded with popular apps, but you might have to search a little more for options. Here are some ways to use your tablet and smartphone in the classroom to offer multisensory learning activities:

- Play popular music for classroom dance breaks
- View interactive e-books
- Play audio books from YouTube.com

- Supplement classroom learning activities for letter, number, and color recognition, phonics, or letter sounds through the use of educational apps
- Incorporate the use of visual and auditory timers

Apps

New apps launch all the time, and it's hard to keep up with all of the best ones. There are many app review sites, such as Common Sense Media (http://www.CommonSenseMedia.org), which include up-to-date lists of the best apps for children, both free and paid, and users can search by specific criteria such as the best apps by age or skill. Common Sense Education (http://www.CommonSense.org/Education) is a website written especially for teachers that is dedicated to educational-technology reviews for apps and websites listed by grade, subject, and platform. Children's Technology Review Exchange or CTREX (http://www.childrenstech.com) shares lists of apps, but a paid monthly subscription is required.

Apps often require frequent software updates by the developer and the end user, so make sure to connect the device to the internet often to use the most up-to-date version and to improve the user experience. Setting aside funds to buy apps can be expensive over time, but April is National Autism Month, so during that month be on the lookout for many developers to offer access to their apps either at no charge or with a substantial discount.

Suggested apps currently available include the following:

- **Breathe, Think, Do with Sesame Street:** This free app is one of my absolute favorites for preschoolers. It features common preschool challenges that lead to frustration, such as being unable to get dressed and put on shoes or share toys. Along with Mando, the Sesame Street character, children are prompted to take deep breaths and to come up with a plan to reduce their anger. Breathe, Think, Do with Sesame Street is available for iPad, iPhone, and Android devices. While it might be helpful to use the app to help a student who is frustrated to learn to take deep breaths when an activity doesn't go his way, this app should also be offered as a learning opportunity for children who are happy and focused, so they can learn an action plan. That way, they will learn appropriate skills to cope with frustration and sensory challenges when they occur.
- **GoNoodle Children's Videos:** GoNoodle is a video collection of fun classroom brain breaks and motor-activity ideas. Short videos include fitness exercises, yoga poses, coordination videos, Kidz Bop dances, Zumba moves, and other indoor recess ideas. Classrooms choose a fun monster and watch it level up with new features every time they play. GoNoodle also has a website with access to similar content and is available on Android and iPad, iPhone, and iPod Touch. GoNoodle is an excellent way for teachers to incorporate whole-class movement during circle time or as brain breaks. There are hundreds of activities included in the app and on the website, which offer teachers tons of options to meet the varying needs of their classroom and students over time.

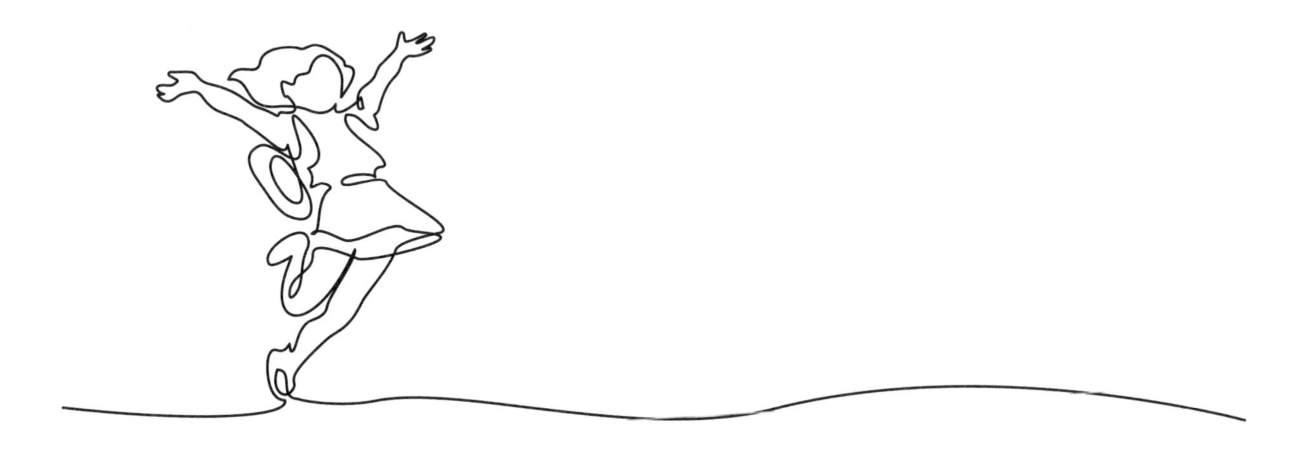

- **First, Then Visual Schedule HD:** Just as the First, Then board strategy can be a helpful tool in the classroom, teachers may benefit by using this app in the classroom to help them develop schedules and choice boards that include pictures, audio-cue recordings, and text. Steps can be timed to keep children on task, and the images can be put in order to help children practice sequences.
- **Time Timer:** Visual timers are helpful for young children to see how much time they have left until they transition. These types of clocks can be purchased for the classroom, but they can be expensive. For only a few dollars, this app offers teachers the opportunity to try out custom timer options to count down time in increments from one minute to an hour. You can select from different alerts, including a tone, an audible sound, or a vibration. Time Timer is available for iPad, iPhone, iPod Touch, and Android devices.
- **Daniel Tiger for Parents App:** This app features the adorable Daniel Tiger from the popular PBS Kids program. It allows parents and teachers to search for clips and songs from the show that they can access on demand to help children process emotions, develop self-control, and learn self-care routines such as getting dressed and using the potty. The Daniel Tiger for Parents app is available for Android, iPad, iPhone, and iPod Touch devices. Preschool-age children adore Daniel Tiger. Many children with sensory processing issues struggle with following through with daily routines and often feel overwhelmed and frustrated. The songs are catchy, the routines are solid, and the educational content is developmentally appropriate for the age group, making this app an easy addition to an early childhood classroom setting.

Alexa and Google Home

For those with access to an Amazon Alexa or Google Home device, a variety of games created to help children move their bodies are available. Use these devices to help set timers and reminders in the classroom, which can aid in more successful transitions. Both devices are able to play a variety of music, which can be fun for children to use their own voices to request their favorite songs to dance to in a brain break. For children who might be struggling to move on after a difficult moment, using Alexa or Google to tell a joke, ask a riddle, or say a tongue twister might be a good distraction to get children back on track.

YouTube Channels

YouTube.com is a video-sharing platform that most children are aware of, because it also serves as a popular entertainment option. The site can be an excellent resource and valuable tool for early childhood educators in their support of children with SPD. Be aware that YouTube also includes ads prior to the start of most videos, and this content should be monitored before you let the children view it. YouTube Children is a safer browsing platform that eliminates the ads and may be better suited for the classroom setting, but not all content available on YouTube.com is available on YouTube Children.

- **Cosmic Children Yoga:** Cosmic Children Yoga offers adorable yoga adventures and mindfulness videos for children that use themed stories with bright illustrations to get children moving their bodies and clearing their minds. There are even *Trolls*-, *Star Wars*-, *Frozen*-, and *Moana*-themed yoga videos, which are free after watching a short video on YouTube. There is an app available for use on iPad, but it includes a costly monthly subscription fee. Yoga poses are an excellent way to offer brain breaks in the classroom or to serve as a transition activity throughout the daily routine.
- **The Learning Station:** The Learning Station offers fun videos and songs for children in their early childhood years that focus on academic concepts, such as counting, using silly voices, and motor actions children will want to imitate.
- **Dr. Jean Feldman:** For more than forty years, "Dr. Jean" has performed educational movement songs that children love, including more than 200 videos for teachers to use as part of their classroom activities. The "Tooty Ta" and "Banana Dance" videos are always popular favorites.
- **Jack Hartmann Kids Music Channel:** This channel offers fun, inspirational musical videos for children. It also offers brain breaks and fitness while learning about letters, numbers, colors, and other early childhood concepts. The entire playlist is dedicated to educational songs that also include American Sign Language (ASL).

Accommodations for Specific Sensory Processing Issues

Accommodations are suggestions or recommendations of what a child might need to be successful in her day-to-day life with sensory issues in a school setting. Accommodations must be listed in public school documents such as IEPs and 504 plans. When a parent signs off on accommodations and services in documents like an IEP or 504, these become legal documents that are enforceable by law. This means that the accommodations must be provided by the personnel instructed to carry them out: teachers, support staff, and therapists. If accommodations are not carried out, the school system could be liable for not providing the supports. Disagreements between parents and the school system can and will happen, especially if it's noticeable that the child is not making effective progress.

While some accommodations can be rather specific, more often than not they are general, to allow for some flexibility in certain areas. Children learn at different rates, and while accommodations can be crucial to a child's success, not all of them work like a magic wand for every child, even for those with similar issues. Therefore, accommodations are often tweaked to allow for some personalization reflective of the child's individual needs.

Private schools and child care where IEPs and 504 plans are not utilized are not required to provide accommodations, but the recommendations in this chapter can offer strategies teachers can use to improve the lives of all of the students in their classroom. This list is comprehensive and is intended to be used as a guideline. The wording of individual accommodations should be left to the school district and the school personnel, to be personalized for individual students and the programs they are attending.

Self-Regulation Accommodations

These accommodations are meant to help children with excess energy to refocus their attention throughout the day in the classroom, during circle time, or through individual activities, to improve their participation.

Provide short, structured motor or exercise breaks at predetermined times throughout the day. Include activities focused on movement and heavy work to assist with self-regulation and attention. For example, children can push the wall, do chair push-ups, or do yoga poses for five- to ten-minute breaks, two to three times per day.

Consider using weighted materials, such as a weighted blanket, toy, or lap pad, during structured learning tasks or during circle time to improve attention and focus.

Consider using a fidget toy during circle time or table work, as long as the student utilizes the fidget item appropriately when learning during teacher instruction. Set up a contract with the student regarding the use of sensory accommodations and how they should be utilized safely and appropriately in the classroom setting.

Offer spatial boundaries and flexible seating during circle time, such as the use of a chair, carpet square, air-filled cushion, or cube chair, to assist with attention and personal space. To improve attention to task, offer flexible seating use, such as a t-stool or air-filled cushion, to improve attention to academic work.

Use a TheraBand positioned on the legs of a desk or table to offer a place to rest the child's feet, while also providing sensory input that may reduce fidgeting in order to stay seated.

Offer alternative work positions for the student, such as allowing her to stand at her desk, sit with a clipboard on a beanbag chair, or complete work in a fashion other than sitting directly in her chair. This approach may help the child to complete nonpreferred academic tasks.

Use calming, preferred sensory activities, such as Kinetic Sand, playdough, or TheraPutty, during breaks to assist with self-regulation.

Consider the use of classroom-related jobs that require heavy work, such as erasing the whiteboard, cleaning tables prior to lunch, delivering reams of paper to the copier station, passing out papers to classmates, placing chairs up on the table at the end of the day, or lifting them down in the morning, as part of structured sensory breaks.

Offer visual demonstrations, skills broken down into smaller tasks, and ample practice opportunities to help the student improve motor planning and learn new skills.

Environmental Accommodations

These accommodations suggest ways to structure the physical classroom setting for children who struggle with sensory processing.

Create a quiet area in the classroom, such as a reading nook or calm-down corner, where a child can be redirected to facilitate self-regulation as needed.

Monitor the classroom environment for the presence of overwhelming visual and auditory stimulation, and reduce overall visual clutter.

Set clear limits and expectations for activities. Visuals may be needed to redirect the student to a required activity if she becomes overstimulated.

Post visual daily classroom schedules and routines for student reference.

Transition Accommodations

These are accommodations to help children leave the classroom or stop doing preferred activities when they must transition to a nonpreferred activity.

Transitional items such as small toys to hold or a sand timer may be helpful when moving on to another activity.

Offer clear, concise directions and expectations with transitions.

Use First, Then boards and statements to help improve compliance for nonpreferred tasks.

Use video modeling to show appropriate classroom expectations.

Use a social story prior to a challenging task to help the child learn new skills and expectations.

Create a personalized schedule for the child to use throughout the school day to aid in transitions.

Use transitional phrases and warnings prior to the end of an activity, paired with an expectation. For example, say, "In five minutes, it's time to get ready to go home." "In three minutes, we will put away the playdough and get our backpacks." "This is a one-minute warning. In one minute, I'll flicker the lights, and you will put your toys in the bin, get your backpack, and return to your seat."

Accommodations for Children with Tactile Sensitivity

These are accommodations for children who are struggling with sensory issues related to touching, playing with, and exploring messy sensory mediums. Teachers should be aware that a student who has difficulty with tactile processing and sensitivities related to tactile mediums generally found in the classroom setting often have an aversion to substances such as shaving cream and paint.

Offer items such as paintbrushes when engaging with nonpreferred tactile mediums to reduce frustration and offer an acceptable solution to encourage play with messy substances.

Monitor the child's position in line when transitioning as a class from one location to another. Let the child be near the front of the line with a teacher. This may help ease transitions and reduce bumping into peers when walking in the hallway.

Fine-Motor Accommodations

Many children struggle with fine-motor skills necessary for appropriately grasping scissors and crayons when completing drawing and writing activities. Fine-motor accommodations may help them improve their pencil grasp and eye-hand coordination.

Offer smaller, fatter writing instruments to support a fingertip grasp pattern.

Encourage the use of utensils, rather than fingers, during snack and meals.

Provide access to a slant board or three-ring binder for writing activities. This may facilitate a fingertip grasp pattern and improve attention to the task.

Offer continued exposure to activities in which children are required to use two hands together, such as stringing beads, writing, and completing puzzles. Use hand-over-hand assistance and visual demonstrations to improve their fine-motor control and eye-hand coordination.

Offer the use of a mechanical pencil to help reduce pencil pressure, as long as it does not frustrate the child if the graphite repeatedly breaks.

Offer multisensory learning opportunities in letter-formation activities, such as writing in sand or forming letters with playdough, to help improve attention.

Accommodations for Picky Eaters

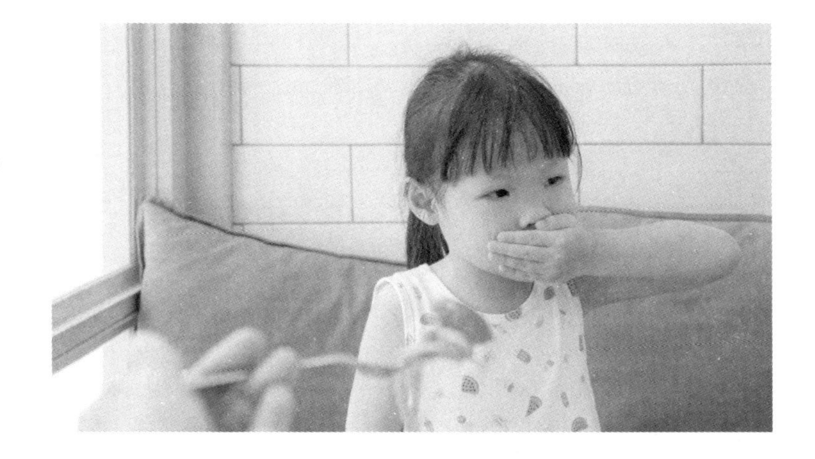

Many children are picky eaters at school, and not eating affects their motor skills for using utensils and their overall health in gaining weight while sustaining their energy levels to perform throughout the day at school. Feeding therapy, in which the student works one on one or in a small group with an occupational therapist or speech therapist in trying new foods, is not generally offered in school. However, many children with sensory issues participate in feeding therapy outside of school, and following through on these recommendations can be beneficial to their skills so they learn to eat foods successfully in different environments. Some children see different foods and are prone to meltdowns and frustration just by looking at nonpreferred foods.

Accommodations for children who picky eaters are not always included in the IEP or 504 plan. These accommodations can be very specific to the child's needs and the district's stance on the matter, but what follows are some general suggestions of accommodations to help support those children who are picky eaters. Parents are often willing to send in different utensils and mealtime items in the child's lunch bag too.

Staff should supervise the child while she is eating, to monitor bite size, if the child overstuffs her mouth when eating and may be at risk for choking during meals and snacks.

Adaptive spoons and forks, or cups with straws or lids, may be required to improve self-feeding during mealtimes.

Show a child a few pictures of different foods that will be offered, and then let her choose one or two foods from those pictures to eat for snack that day.

Playground Accommodations

The playground is a fun place where most children with sensory issues can get their energy out appropriately, but it can also be a source of frustration due to transitions. Here are some recommended accommodations for children who require playground assistance to support their sensory needs at school. Note that recess and playground time are important for self-regulation and should not be used as a punishment or taken away from the student for any reason.

Continuing to offer a structured activity rather than free play upon transition into the playground may assist with self-regulation and avoid overstimulation. For example, engage the student in follow-the-leader-type games or obstacle courses to offer structured sensory input as needed.

Prior to leaving the playground, encourage the student to engage in yoga poses or a short, stationary exercise routine as a transitional tool to return to the classroom setting.

Monitor the student in the classroom and on the playground to compensate for poor safety awareness and occasional or frequent lack of visual attention.

Accommodations for Children with Auditory Hypersensitivity

The sounds in a classroom setting can be overwhelming for many students and can lead to stress, anxiety, and fight-or-flight behaviors. Many accommodations are designed to help students who are overwhelmed with noise in the classroom and in large-group activities.

Offer access to noise-cancelling headphones to dampen and reduce extraneous noise in a busy classroom environment. These can also work well for community locations such as the auditorium or cafeteria.

Offer preferential seating in loud, busy environments as far away from the sound source as is practical.

Monitor the classroom environment for the presence of overwhelming visual and auditory stimulation.

If possible, forewarn the student of upcoming fire drills.

Consider providing the student with a quiet, distraction-free workspace to reduce stress over environmental sounds.

Accommodations for Children Who Seek Oral Sensory Input

Chewing on shirts and other nonfood items in the classroom can be unsafe for young children. Many children with sensory issues need access to a safe way to seek oral sensory input to satisfy their craving and to assist with self-regulation and attention.

Redirect oral seeking through chewing on clothing and other classroom items by allowing the use of preferred food items, including Tic Tacs, strong mints, or gum (provided by parents).

The student may benefit from the use of oral sensory fidgets in the classroom during seated work. Consider providing chewable jewelry or chewy fidgets, with teacher supervision, as needed.

A sport-top water bottle, provided by the parent, may be helpful to redirect the need for oral stimulation seeking in the classroom setting.

Providing a Sensory-Friendly Classroom on a Limited Budget

When building your classroom library of sensory items, it's best to find items that appeal to a broad population of children at first. Then, over time, add to it with more specific items. For teachers who are looking to expand their personal access to tools that could be beneficial for children with sensory issues, here are some ways to help build up your resources. Don't think that a child has to have sensory issues to benefit from the recommended items. Many of these sensory tools are beneficial for all students, not just those who tend to struggle more than others.

Ask for gift cards and create item wish lists. Many teachers create lists of preferred items using Amazon wish lists. Many parents are gracious and willing to buy supplies, so it's worth asking. Consider forgoing individual teacher gifts during the holidays. Instead, ask parents to donate items from your wish list. Or ask for Amazon or iTunes gift cards to purchase items and apps on your own.

Write grant proposals to local funding sources. While there are national grants available for teachers who are willing to do research or participate in special programs, there may be an opportunity to secure local funding from special programs in the district or through a parent advisory board or PTO. Plan to apply every year, as there are always new items to purchase, and over time seat cushions will deflate or items will get misused or misplaced.

Use crowdfunding sites. Crowdfunding sites like DonorsChoose.org and GoFundMe.com can be great ways to tap into friends, family members, and others in the community who might be willing to donate a few dollars toward items such as fidget toys, flexible seating, and sensory activities. DonorsChoose.org is a website entirely dedicated to funding classroom projects. Teachers create and post about classroom projects. Many people who are looking to support education projects in a defined geographic area use this website to find and, often anonymously, donate to unique causes. GoFundMe is another option for raising money, but a certain percentage of the money raised pays GoFundMe for use of the site and its materials; that overhead might be a determining factor when trying to raise money.

Search yard sales, including virtual yard sales. While it can be hard to find the time to go from one yard sale to another, apps and websites are revolutionizing private sales. Virtual yard sale groups on Facebook, Facebook Marketplace, NextDoor, and Craigslist are all ways to post items you might be looking for, or a quick way to purchase someone's leftover exercise ball for a fraction of its original price. However, always exercise caution when planning to meet a stranger to buy or sell something. Also, at the beginning and end of each school year, or if they are moving to a new classroom, many teachers liquidate resources they no longer use and are glad to pass them on to others inexpensively.

Closing Thoughts

> Children will do well if they can.
>
> —Ross Greene, PhD

As an occupational therapist who is part of an educational team, I've sat in meetings at conference tables within local school districts, then left the building to finish work at the end of the day in a clinical hospital setting. There are pros and cons to working with children in these different settings, and the experiences have provided a more well-rounded understanding of the struggles that both parents and teachers face when trying to help children with sensory issues succeed throughout their day. Knowing what is expected in each situation is crucial, because each environment has its own set of rules and expectations. It can be hard for parents to understand why certain accommodations or expectations that are helpful to the child at home or in a clinic cannot be provided for their child at school. Some children are not eligible for school services at all, because they might not be showing enough of a delay in their development, even though they are clearly struggling. These types of frustrations tend to happen a lot, especially as insurance companies have become less likely to approve intervention, and parents are faced with expensive deductibles and copays that make outpatient services cost prohibitive.

This is why knowing your role as a teacher is very important, so that the discussions you have with parents and the recommendations you make for the child in the school setting are appropriate for the environment. Too often, the guidelines do not provide students with every resource they could benefit from. Children are entitled to a free and appropriate public education—not the *best* free and appropriate education—a nuance that can be frustrating and upsetting for everyone. Educate yourself on roles and responsibilities as part of the team you are on, and if you have doubts, ask administrators to help you decide what's within your scope of practice and the role of the facility.

If a child is exhibiting challenging behaviors, then there is something that the child is struggling with. Be the child's eyes and ears in the classroom; put yourself in his shoes. Ask yourself what could be causing him to react. Is it the environment? another student? Think about what you could do differently to make the classroom a happier place for him, so he can learn to love learning. Children with sensory issues have needs that can change from one minute to the next. They need people to love and care for them despite their challenges. Teachers who are willing to try new things in the classroom and advocate for their students become trusted allies for students, parents, and other teachers too. Believe that all children are capable. Do not blame a child, parent, or home setting for the child's behavior. Children are part of families. Many families are struggling with something, and while the environment can absolutely contribute to a child's positive or negative participation on any given day, it's possible the classroom environment is more than he can handle. There are ways to help children to feel and be successful. Leave the medication and difficult stuff up to the physicians, and know that you have the power to help, with the accommodations, strategies, effort, and compassion you show that student each day in your classroom.

Think of the accommodations and strategies in this book simply as good teaching practices you might not have known about yet. Diagnoses can be incorrect and can change over time as students get older and teachers and parents gain more information about their learning style. While there are similarities and predictions that can be made over time for children who exhibit similar behaviors, no one person or story is identical to the next. The best teachers show empathy, are willing to help, and offer support and constructive feedback to help a child's education. Instead of making lists of problems and pointing out challenges, they offer solutions and a genuine willingness to help when problems arise.

Checking your own emotional baggage at the door is important, because children with sensory issues will sense your emotions and react to them. Your attitude can also affect how you respond. Children with sensory issues need love, care, comfort, patience, and understanding—just like every other child. Spend time trying to understand what the children are struggling with, and regardless of their diagnoses, try to employ a strategy to see if it helps. But don't offer a strategy once and wonder why it didn't magically work. Children with sensory issues do not like change, and many of these strategies need to be provided slowly and consistently over time. Observe a child's actions and reactions, and really listen to the words he shares. Most children are able to offer valuable feedback to their teachers on how something makes them feel.

Sometimes sensory needs get worse before they get better. This happens when we're trying to change challenging behaviors. If things get difficult, you have valuable information to share with the family and other educators that will help make future programming the best it can be for that child and the students who follow. Moreover, you will have educated other professionals along the way. Ideally, together you will stumble on a solution that can change the trajectory of the child's educational and academic experience for the better.

Appendix: Websites and Resources

GoNoodle (https://www.gonoodle.com/) is a website that houses a huge quantity of free videos to use during sensory breaks and brain breaks for the entire classroom or individual children. Users get a fun monster who levels up and gains different accessories the more time is spent in the app.

Common Sense Media (https://www.commonsensemedia.org/) provides free reviews of movies, apps, and websites that are written for parents and shares all the information parents and teachers will want to know about media before showing it to children, such as whether there is inappropriate content or how to talk through challenging themes.

Common Sense Education (https://www.commonsense.org/education/) includes advice for teachers on promoting literacy, digital citizenship, and other technology resources in the classroom with app and website reviews that include an educational-technology focus.

Understood (http://understood.org/) is a website and resource for parents of children with ADHD and other learning disabilities. The organization produces articles and shares relevant information about 504 plans and IEPs while offering access to experts such as therapists, psychologists, and educators; parents, caregivers, and teachers can ask personal and pertinent questions in safe forums through podcasts and other social media avenues such as Facebook and Twitter.

Lesson Pix (https://lessonpix.com/) For a small monthly subscription fee, Lesson Pix allows teachers and parents to use clip art to quickly create custom visuals for the classroom or for individual students to post routines, label shelves, or design First, Then boards and social stories.

PBS Kids (https://pbskids.org/) includes videos and games featuring popular PBS characters such as Curious George, Dinosaur Train, and Daniel Tiger's Neighborhood. Printable downloads are included with many of the activities.

Pinterest (https://www.pinterest.com/) is a popular website and app that allows users to find great resources using a specific search topic and to "pin" the discoveries to organized virtual boards. Users create custom boards, such as Classroom Storage, Sensory Toys, and Seating, and pin articles there for use as reference later on. Pinterest is an easy way to help organize classroom resources such as printable downloads or to search for new strategies such as fun ways to organize the classroom or do-it-yourself tutorials on how to make popular sensory items.

Etsy (https://www.etsy.com/) is a popular website to visit when looking to buy homemade items from others, such as custom weighted blankets, fidget toys, beanbags, sensory boxes, floor paths, sensory bottles, busy boards, themed sensory bin items, rainbow rice, scented homemade dough, wooden toys, and so forth. Make sure to read reviews before purchasing these custom gifts. Shipping charges may apply.

The Genius of Play (https://www.thegeniusofplay.org/) is an excellent resource for parents and teachers looking for simple activities to do in the classroom; lesson plan ideas; current research and reports regarding play; and take-home pages to send home to parents, all of which can help develop the valuable educational skills children learn through play.

Lives In the Balance (https://www.livesinthebalance.org/) is a nonprofit organization founded by Dr. Ross Greene that shares tools and strategies for parents and teachers to engage successfully with children with challenging behavior through empathy and collaborative problem solving.

Printable Download Websites

Teachers Pay Teachers, Tools to Grow, Your Therapy Source, and Pre-K Pages are just a few of the excellent websites available on the internet where teachers can search for downloadable worksheets and classroom resources to print, such as routines and classroom pictures to label shelving. Many resources are free, but others might cost a few dollars for access to download.

Therapy Tools

Amazon.com is a popular website to buy therapy tools. Therapro, Southpaw, Abilitations, Pocket Full of OT, Fun and Function, Oriental Trading, Stacy's Sensory Solutions, Lakeshore Learning, Fat Brain Toys, and SportTime (School Specialty) are websites on which to look for cool toys, fidget items, weighted items, flexible seating, motor equipment, and other useful tools for the classroom. Don't forget to peruse dollar stores and party aisles, where you can find fun fidgets and sensory items too.

References

American Psychiatric Association. 2013. *Diagnostic and Statistical Manual of Mental Disorders*. 5th edition (DSM-5). Arlington, VA: American Psychiatric Association.

Ayres, A. Jean, and Jeff Robbins. 1979. *Sensory Integration and the Child*. Los Angeles, CA: Western Psychological Services.

Chang, Yi-Shin, et al. 2016. "White Matter Microstructure Is Associated with Auditory and Tactile Processing in Children with and without Sensory Processing Disorder." *Frontiers in Neuroanatomy* 9: 169. https://www.frontiersin.org/articles/10.3389/fnana.2015.00169/full#h8

Greene, Ross. 2016. *Raising Human Beings: Creating a Collaborative Partnership with Your Child*. New York, NY: Scribner.

Individuals with Disabilities Education Improvement Act of 2004. Pub. L. No. 108-446, 118 Stat. 2647.

Kuypers, Leah. 2011. *Zones of Regulation: A Curriculum Designed to Foster Self-Regulation and Emotional Control*. Santa Clara, CA: Think Social.

Lee, Andrew M. I. 2019. "Individuals With Disabilities Education Act (IDEA): What You Need to Know." Understood. https://www.understood.org/en/school-learning/your-childs-rights/basics-about-childs-rights/individuals-with-disabilities-education-act-idea-what-you-need-to-know

Miller, Lucy Jane. 2014. *Sensational Children: Hope and Help for Children with Sensory Processing Disorder (SPD)*. Rev. ed. New York, NY: Perigee.

Morin, Amanda. 2019. "Developmental Delays: What You Need To Know." Understood. https://www.understood.org/en/learning-attention-issues/treatments-approaches/early-intervention/what-you-need-to-know-about-developmental-delays

Morin, Amanda. 2019. "Heavy Work and Sensory Processing Issues: What You Need To Know." Understood. https://www.understood.org/en/learning-attention-issues/child-learning-disabilities/sensory-processing-issues/heavy-work-activities

Morin, Amanda. 2019. "Interoception and Sensory Processing Issues: What You Need To Know." Understood. https://www.understood.org/en/learning-attention-issues/child-learning-disabilities/sensory-processing-issues/interoception-and-sensory-processing-issues-what-you-need-to-know

NAEYC. 2012. "Technology and Interactive Media as Tools in Early Childhood Programs Serving Children Birth through Age 8." Position statement. Washington, DC: NAEYC. https://www.naeyc.org/sites/default/files/globally-shared/downloads/PDFs/resources/topics/PS_technology_WEB.pdf

Owen, Julia, et al. 2013. "Abnormal White Matter Microstructure in Children with Sensory Processing Disorders." Neuroimage: Clinical. 2: 844–853. https://www.sciencedirect.com/science/article/pii/S2213158213000776?via%3Dihub

Star Institute for Sensory Processing Disorder. 2018. "Understanding Sensory Processing Disorder." Star Institute. https://www.spdstar.org/basic/understanding-sensory-processing-disorder

US Department of Health and Human Services, Office for Civil Rights. 2006. *Fact Sheet: Your Rights Under Section 504 of the Rehabilitation Act*. Washington, DC: Department of Health and Human Services. https://www.hhs.gov/sites/default/files/ocr/civilrights/resources/factsheets/504.pdf

Wilbarger, P. L., and Julia L. Wilbarger. 2007. *Sensory Defensiveness: A Comprehensive Treatment Approach*. Rev. ed. Panorama City, CA: Avanti Educational Programs.

Williams, M. S., and Sherry Shellenberger. 1996. *How Does Your Engine Run? A Leader's Guide to the Alert Program for Self-Regulation*. Albuquerque, NM: Therapyworks.

Index